The Political Aspects of
St. Augustine's "City of God"

John Neville Figgis

The Political Aspects of St. Augustine's "City of God"

Copyright © 2023 Indo-European Publishing

The present edition is a reproduction of previous publication of this classic work. Minor typographical errors may have been corrected without note; however, for an authentic reading experience the spelling, punctuation, and capitalization have been retained from the original text.

ISBN: 979-8-88942-191-7

CONTENTS

PREFACE

THE delivery of these lectures was one of the last pieces of work that Neville Figgis was allowed to carry through. He prepared them for the press, leaving them in the form of lectures and preserving here and there the impress which the anxiety of war-crisis made upon them. In that form, therefore, they are published now. In place of the final revision which his failing health prevented him from making, another hand has tried unskilfully to supply what he would have done with skill, in order to carry out his wishes and make his last complete piece of work accessible to a wider public than those who heard the lectures delivered.

MIRFIELD, *ALL Saints' Day,* 1920

GENERAL SCOPE OF THE 'DE CIVITATE DEI'

'As Man amongst creatures and the Church amongst men and the Fathers in the Church, and S. Augustine amongst the Fathers, so amongst the many pretious volumes and in the rich storehouse of his workes, his bookes of the City of God have a speciall preheminence.'

So W. Crashawe began the dedication which he prefixed in 1620 to the second edition of J. Healey's translation of the text and of the Commentary thereon of J. L. Vives. Vives had dedicated his Commentary to Henry VIII, dating from Louvain on July 7, 1522.

This passage of Crashawe we might parallel from writers of almost every age; and from some of widely different outlook. Bishop Otto of Freising, the uncle and historian of Frederic Barbarossa, sings in unison with Niceron, the collector of literary anecdotes in the seventeenth century.

The greatness of the 'De Civitate Dei' is not in dispute. No student of the fifth century can afford to overlook it. No one can understand the Middle Ages without taking it into account. What is true of historians is true no less of ecclesiastical politicians and reformers—even down to a leader in the modern socialist movement like Sommerlad.[1] In his earlier days Count Hertling has written on the book, and he alluded to its principles in a recent speech. The book has been more widely read than any other of S. Augustine except the 'Confessions.' It has had commentators from Coquaeus down to Scholz. For these reasons it might seem hardly a fitting topic for 'Pringle-Stewart' lectures. One historian said to me on hearing of the

1

Course: 'Is there anything new to say about that?' Yet another said, that the more he tried to comprehend the mind of the Middle Ages, the more was he convinced that it was necessary to understand S. Augustine.

That understanding is not easy. There are those who are for treating S. Augustine as the typical example of the medieval temperament with its heights and depths, its glories and splendours of imagination, its dialectical ingenuity and its irrational superstitions. Others see in S. Augustine essentially a man of the antique world. They do not deny to him real influence upon later times. Who can? But they are inclined to minimise this; at least in matters of social and political importance. The former is the view of Dorner, still more of Feuerlein.[2] It became a commonplace with scholars like Gierke and Ritschl, and in a less degree with Harnack. It is presented in an extreme form in a book, once well known, that came from America, the late Dr. A. V. G. Alien's ' Continuity of Christian Thought.' Hermann Reuter in his 'Augustinische Studien' began a reaction. That book is of incalculable value for those who wish to comprehend S. Augustine. This reaction reached its limit in a book published during the war, by Troeltsch, 'Die christliche Antike und die Mittelalter.' Signs of this view are to be found in Dr. Carlyle's valuable work on 'Political Theory in the West'—although it is more through what he does not say than what he does, that we gather the views of the writer. Professor Dunning in his 'History of Political Thought' is even more significant in his omissions.

Political thought and S. Augustine's influence thereon are to be the topic of these lectures. That involves the whole subject of Church and State. So we are carried some way into theology. The ' De Civitate Dei' is not a treatise on politics. It is a *lime de circonstance* concerned with apologetic. Most of S. Augustine's doctrine alike in theology and philosophy is embedded in it. We may regard it as an expansion of the 'Confessions.' The relation of true philosophy to scepticism, the idea of creation, the problem of time, the contribution of Platonism, more especially Neo-Platonism, the meaning of miracle and nature, the Incarnation as expressing the humility of God, the whole scheme of redemption, salvation by grace, long divagations into

2

comparative mythology, all these might be made the subject of lectures on the 'De Civitate Dei,' and that without leaving the *terrain* occupied by the author. Another lecturer better equipped might give not six but twelve lectures concerning the philosophic and theological problems suggested by the 'De Civitate Dei,' and not even mention those points which I hope to discuss. If that had been what was expected, you would not have done me the high honour of choosing me to lecture on this work. To begin with, a great Augustinian scholar, Canon T. A. Lacey, in the first course of 'Pringle-Stewart' lectures discussed some of the more important of these matters, although without special reference to this book. You would not wish them discussed again by one who has neither Mr. Lacey's intimate knowledge of S. Augustine nor his alertness of critical judgment. So I shall limit myself to the political aspects of the book.

The points which it offers to the student of political thought are not few, nor are they unimportant. The book has been treated as a philosophy of history finer than that of Hegel; and again as the herald of all that is significant in the 'Scienza Nuova' of Vico. Can such views be sustained? Or is it the case that S. Augustine had no notion of a philosophy of history, that his views are self-contradictory, and that only a few passages throw more than a faint light on it. That question will form the topic of the second lecture. Did S. Augustine teach, that the State is the organisation of sin, or did he believe in its God given character, and desire its developments? Did he teach the political supremacy of the hierarchy, and, by implication, that of the Pope and the Inquisition? Or was it of the Church as the *Communio sanctorum* that he was thinking? Does his doctrine of individual election reduce to ruins all ecclesiastical theory? These topics will occupy the third and fourth lectures. What was S. Augustine's influence on mediæval life? Was there something almost like a 'reception' of Augustinianism, followed by a repudiation at the Renaissance? Or was it that only slightly he affected political ideals in the Middle Ages? Some see the whole controversy between Popes and Emperors implicit in the 'De Civitate Dei.' Others would trace it to causes quite different. What real change came about at the Reformation? Did S. Augustine's social doctrine (apart from the theology of grace) lose all influence? Or did men retain unimpaired the idea of the *civitas Dei,* as it had been developed? These questions will occupy the last two lectures.

To-day let me try to determine certain preliminary points. Let us get clear what is the nature and aim of the book. Much needs to be said which will seem trite to students. I would crave your pardon. These matters are needful for evidence of what will later be said. Besides, it is a less error to take too little for granted than too much.

Like nearly all of S. Augustine's writings, the 'De Civitate Dei' is controversial. It is a pamphlet of large scale. Like S. Paul and unlike S. Thomas, Augustine wrote only under the pressure of immediate necessity. All his writings have an apologetic character. Most of them are coloured by his intensely rich personality. Trained in rhetoric, Augustine is never abstract or impersonal. Sometimes we regret this and the *longueurs* to which his skill in dialectic leads him. Theories abound in S. Augustine's works, but the last thing he is is a theorist, pure and simple. Augustine became a theologian, as he had become a philosopher, driven by practical needs. Adversaries might even argue that all his emphasis on the external, on the given quality of grace, was due to his own experiences—just as Luther universalised his own inner life into the doctrine of justification by faith. We must see the place which these controversies, implied in the 'De Civitate,' occupied in S. Augustine's life. After his conversion, he spent the first years in assailing the doctrines of which he had been an adherent. We have the books 'Contra Academicos,' the 'Soliloquy' and other writings against the Manichæans. In these he is concerned with problems mainly speculative, the nature and origin of evil, the nature of belief, the possibility of certitude, the significance of error, which at least is evidence of the personality of the man in error, and so forth.

To these controversies succeeded his great conflict with the Donatists. When he was converted, Augustine did not become a merely intellectual adherent of Christianity. He became a member of a visible, active and world-wide Church; and that in a day of storms. When Augustine came home to Africa, after his

4

mother's death, he found the Church rent by schism, with the Catholics appearing as the weaker party, and the Donatists claiming almost a national position. Augustine was forced into the position of a champion of the Catholic Church. Consequently, more in regard to schism than to heresy, he developed the idea of the unity and universality of the Church. He thus marked a difference between himself and Greek theologians like Origen.

Then came the sack of Rome by Alaric. Only in our own time can the shock of that world-catastrophe be paralleled in its effect on the imagination and thoughts of men. The eternity of Rome had been a presupposition of the common consciousness. But now the world seemed in ruins—*i.e.* the world of imagination and mental comfort. Augustine saw that the taking of Rome had no 'great military significance.' In one sermon he bids his hearers be calm and recollect that Rome really means Romans—and that the Roman name was not extinguished. The calamity gave its last chance to dying paganism. Rome had been a stronghold of the ancient worship, and was still largely pagan in feeling. Obvious then was its line of counterattack. 'This horror would not have been, had we stood by the ancient ways. The mad policy of the Emperors in prohibiting sacrifices to the gods has produced its inevitable nemesis. The sack of Rome is the judgment of Jove.'

This was the position in which Augustine was placed, one somewhat resembling that of a modern Christian faced with the charge that Christianity is bankrupt because it did not prevent the war. To meet the charge Augustine wrote the 'De Civitate Dei.' He did not write it all at once. In the 'Retractations' he admits that he was interrupted by the Pelagian controversy. That too leaves its traces upon this encyclopedia of his mind. Much of the book is but an expansion of Augustine's doctrine of grace applied on the scale of world history. That is another reason why the book is so hard. Augustine had a discursive mind, and his training in rhetoric increased this tendency. He had no great powers of construction. The architectonics even of the 'Confessions' leave much to be desired—a fact which is less patent than it should be to many because they do not read the latter books. In his controversial writings he does not know when to stop; nor does he trouble much about relevance. We can never understand S. Augustine if we think of him as a system-maker. Systems may have come out of him, but before all else he is a personality. He is the meeting-place of two worlds. All that the training of that day in the West could give—he knew little or no Greek—he had. His mind was a mould into which the culture of the world was poured. This he had either to assimilate to Christianity, or to eliminate from himself. Sometimes he is inclined to do the latter. Hence his inconsistencies; and in consequence many different people could justify themselves out of his writings. Augustine is not, as some think, a pure ascetic without interest in human life, careless of the goods of learning—but sometimes he seems to be that. He is a rich, hot-blooded, highly complex and introspective personality, passionately Christian, but exquisitely and delicately human, sensitive and courageous, looking with reverence on Rome, possessed, with Virgil and Cicero, of a Roman love of authority and law, and an African touch of earth, yet ever withal having the *nostalgia of the infinite*. Within Augustine there struggle two personalities, a mystic, who could forgo all forms, not only of outward but of inward mechanism, and fly straight—'the alone to the Alone' —with a champion of ecclesiastical order, resolute to secure the rights of the Church, and a statesman looking before and after.

One constant temptation besets the historian of thought in every sphere. He is apt to suppose that his subjects are more consistent than they are; to make logical wholes of scattered and often contradictory hints; and sometimes even to rule out, as unauthentic, writings which have no other evidence against them than that of being hard to reconcile with others of the same author. In no case could this be a worse error than in that of S. Augustine; in no part of S. Augustine could it be worse than in the 'De Civitate Dei.' One student has said: 'It is not a book, it is journalism; whenever S. Augustine had nothing else to do he sat down and wrote a bit of it.' That may be fancy. But it is a fanciful way of conveying a truth. Let us then take the work right through, and give an account of it, not troubling about its logical consistency or the relevance of parts to the main idea.

In the 'Retractations' Augustine gave his own analysis of it, though a very brief one. The first five books are a reply to those who say that the pagan gods are to be worshipped for the sake of earthly security and peace. The next five are a reply to the contention of the philosophic apologists that the worship of old Roman gods leads to the real good, eternal life. The pagans having been routed, Augustine turned to construction. This is divided into three parts. In Books XI-XIV we have the origin of the two cities, the *Civitas Dei* and the *Civitas terrena*; in the next four he traces their course in time, and in the last four their consummation in eternity.

Let us go through the work in further detail. In Book I, Augustine states that his object in writing is to rebut the charge that Christianity has ruined Rome. He shows that temporal felicity had not been the unvarying condition for the city of Rome. Besides, the same gods had failed to protect Troy, or else Æneas would never have reached Italy. Even at the time of writing, Christianity, he claims, is having its effect, in getting better treatment for the vanquished. Pagans— the very men who attack the Church—go running to the churches to take sanctuary. There they are safe. Augustine does not claim that a complete acceptance of Christianity would guarantee the life of a nation.

The laments over a toppling order, he will not meet by saying that a Christian commonwealth now or at any future date will be stable. What marks this book is the final repudiation of the old views, as much Jewish as pagan, that temporal felicity follows the service of the true God—alike for the individual and the nation.

The wicked, either man or nation, may flourish like a green bay tree, says S. Augustine, and often will. That will not advantage the wicked in the end, which is outside this life. But it will teach the good man humility and a due dependence on the eternal values. The world may be saved. But it will be saved on other-worldly lines. Hermann Reuter is right in saying that the whole world turns on the contrast between worldly and other-worldly motives.[3]

7

Augustine replies to the charge against the Christians by a doctrine concerning the nature of religion which makes the topic of temporal felicity irrelevant. This method was a revolution. Like most of S. Augustine's thought—and some of Christian teaching—it was neither entirely novel nor exclusively Christian. It rests on the philosophic conception of God as the *summum bonum.* 'What is the chief end of man? To glorify God and to enjoy Him for ever.' This may be a summary of the Christian ideal, but it includes within it the Neo-Platonist also and many others. Augustine was aware of this, and in the second part he will meet and refute the argument that eternal goods are to be won by the worship of the pagan deities. Meanwhile he is occupied with those who complain of the evil wrought by Christianity. Against them he points out the luxury and corruption of Rome, all the ills predicted by Scipio if Carthage should be destroyed and Jeshurun wax fat with that lust of sovereignty which among all other sins of the world was most appropriate unto the Romans. He depicts the tragedies produced by the lust of power describes the hideous sexualities current in the theatre and in certain worships not yet discarded, despite all the Gothic peril. He concludes by sketching his plan to point out (1) the evils that befel Rome in early days; (2) the uselessness, so proved, of the old gods even for temporal ends; (3) their even greater uselessness for eternal bliss.

The second book is mainly concerned with the profound moral gulf between paganism and Christianity. Therein Augustine makes lavish use of the 'De Republica' of Cicero. He describes in detail the decay of Roman manners during the last days of the Republic, glancing at the moral and political passions which preceded and provoked the Imperial regime. This book is designed to establish the now familiar thesis of the moral and political corruption produced by paganism, and concludes with an exhortation to the Romans to renounce it.

Book III describes the miseries that ushered in and accompanied the triumphs of Rome. With these are contrasted the golden times of peace under King Numa and the wickedness of the attack on Alba Longa. Emphasis is thus laid on the

8

miseries inherent in the pagan state as an expression of pagan ethics and religion.

In Book IV Augustine lays down that justice is to be set before power, and that alike by by nations and individuals. We come to the maxim on which so much more must be said: *Remota justitia, quid regna nisi magna latrocinia.* The Roman Empire he seems on the whole to have viewed as a just reward earned partly as the due of Roman virtue and partly in compensation for unjust attacks; but he is not always consistent. He speaks of the lust of power of Ninus and the Assyrian Empire. Here we come in Chapters 3 and 15 to strongly anti-imperialist passages. Thence Augustine proceeds (C. 11) to consider the more refined forms of paganism— those which take the individual deities as names for the attributes of the one supreme God who was often interpreted pantheistically. He decides that Jove was at least no final organiser of victory for his children, and in that noteworthy passage (IV, 15) he argues in favour of a society of small States, 'little in quantity and peaceful in neighbourly agreement,' as against the aggregations of empire. Once more he makes easy game of the puerilities of polytheism, and denounces its obscene festivals. Thence he passes to the more serious doctrine of Varro, for whom Augustine entertained the greatest respect. Acute and learned, with a prodigious memory, Varro is Augustine's main authority for mythology— just as later on Vico, who knew Varro mainly through the 'De Civitate Dei,' is driven at every turn to appeal to him. Varro was a Theist or Pantheist of a kind, and like Augustine worshipped a Providence, the bestower of kingdoms, who grants his boons to bad no less than good, like a parent giving toys. The book concludes with the assertion that God is the giver of all kingdoms and the determiner of their end, and with illustrations drawn from the Jewish State.

Book V enters into the problem of freedom and necessity. Despite his strong predestinarian doctrine Augustine was no believer in a blind fate—any more than was Calvin. Empire he holds, has been given to the Romans as the reward of certain terrestrial virtues. Great qualities of courage and self-sacrifice belong or did belong to Roman patriots. No pagan could be more eloquent than he is on their grandeur. He will even set them as an example for the citizens of the heavenly city. 'The argonauts of the ideal' are bidden to emulate the zeal and sacrifice which Romans had shown for a cause so far inferior. The well-known passage from the sixth Æneid, *excudent alii spirantia mollius aera,* is used to illustrate Roman imperialism (V, 12). Augustine argues that ambition may be a vice, but that it acts in restraint.

of worse vices, cowardice and indolence. Even here the Christian martyr is superior. He despised earthly honours and endured worse torments. The Romans had not the true end of doing God's will. Hence they could have no eternal hope. Their relative goodness would have gone unrewarded, and God's justice therefore would for ever be assailable, had not an earthly sovereignty been their meed. That species of power is other in kind than the eternal joy of the children of God. Yet once more must Augustine assert that it is the true God who gave Rome her Empire and who presides over the origin and issue of all wars. There he anticipates the argument of Dante. Rhadagaisus, the Gothic king, whom they all know, forms a shining example of this divine supervision in his sudden and incalculable downfall.

Following this passage is the famous *Fürsten-spiegel,* the picture of a godly prince (V, 24). Somewhat to our surprise, Augustine chooses as an instance Constantine the Great. Maybe he knew less ill of him than we do. At least this choice shows how entirely Roman was Augustine. Theodosius the Great is then made the topic of a panegyric, for he grudged not to assist the labouring Church by all the wholesome laws which he promulgated against heretics.

Augustine's first part concludes with Book V. He is now to be occupied in showing that paganism is wrong even as a method of approach to the True God.

Vulgar paganism is now demolished. We pass in Book VI to the philosophic creeds. An interesting appreciation of Varro precedes an account of his book on 'Human and Divine Antiquities' which indeed we know largely through the use Augustine makes of it. Varro divides religion into three stages,

10

somewhat after the manner of Comte. There is *(a)* the mythical, followed by *(b)* the natural and *(c)* the civic. He prefers the second. Augustine tries to show the connexion between the two, and denies that paganism can be detached from its darker side. It is vain to worship pagan deities in the hope of eternal bliss. Book VII carries the matter a little further, and argues the inconsistency of Varro.

Book VIII treats of the Platonic doctrine of God. This in the main Augustine accepts; but he treats as futile the attempt to accommodate it with the worship of the pagan pantheon. Apuleius, the African representative of paganism, is discussed. We have vigorous words in abuse of magic. The heathen practice of apotheosis is contrasted with the honours given to the Christian martyr. This, he says, is high reverence, but in no sense do we treat the martyrs as gods. Book IX is concerned with a further condemnation of the doctrine of mediating spirits and demons. Thence Augustine passes to the doctrine of the One Mediator, and argues the possibility of the Incarnation. The Book shows that the debate between the Christian apologist and his assailants is at bottom a conflict between two forms of mediation.

Book X contains a further analysis of Plotinus, whose doctrine Augustine parallels with the Logos doctrine of S. John i. He contrasts the one sacrifice, once offered, with the offerings to idols; and the Christian with the pagan miracles. In Chapter 25 he argues that all good men in every age are saved, but saved through faith in Christ, *e.g.* the saints of the Old Testament. Then we have more argument for the Incarnation. Augustine sees the fundamental difficulty in Incarnation, a self-limitation of God which is all but intolerable. It is this doctrine of the humility of God at which imagination boggles. 'These proud fellows scorn to have God for their Master, because the Word became Flesh and dwelt among us.'

The last words of Book X sum up the first part of the whole:

'In these ten books I have spoken by the good assistance of God sufficient in sound judgments (though some expected more) against the impious contradictors that prefer their gods before the founder of the holy city, whereof we are to dispute. The first five of the ten opposed them that adored their gods for temporal respects; the five later against those that adored them for the life to come. It remains now, according as we promised in the first book, to proceed in our discourse of the two cities that are confused together in this world, and distinct in the other; of whose original, progress, and consummation I now enter to dispute, evermore invoking the assistance of the Almighty.'

Now at last in Book XI we get to the two cities. Augustine begins by proving that the universe and time began together. The City of God begins with the creation of light, *i.e.* with the angels; and the other with the sin of Satan. The doctrine of the Trinity is expounded, and Augustine emphasises his view that evil is a defect of will, not of nature, once more attacking the Manichæan dualism. 'Let there be light' signifies the creation of the angelic hierarchy.

Book XII once more discusses the relations of the good and evil angels. Augustine meets and denies the doctrine of the longevity of the world, of the Antipodes, of an eternal recurrence. He goes on to the creation of man. Book XIII describes the fall, and its consequence in death. He combats the view that death was inevitable, not penal. In Book XIV we proceed to the ordinary doctrine of the irruption of grace. After dilating on the evils of sin, he describes the two cities more at large in Chapter 28.

'Two loves therefore have given original to these two cities—self-love in contempt of God unto the earthly; love of God in contempt of one's self to the heavenly. The first seeks the glory of men and the latter desires God only as the testimony of conscience, the greatest glory. That glories in itself, and this in God. That exalts itself in self-glory; this says to God, "My glory, the lifter of my head." That boasts of the ambitious conquerors, led by the lust of sovereignty: in this everyone serves the other in charity, both the rulers in counselling and the subjects in obeying. That loves worldly virtue in the potentates; this says unto God, "I will love thee, O Lord, my strength." And the wise men of that follow either the good things of the body or mind or both, living according to the flesh, and such as might know God

12

honoured him not as God, nor were thankful, but all were vain in their own imaginations, and their foolish heart was darkened; for professing themselves to be wise— that is, extolling themselves proudly in their own wisdom— they became fools, changing the glory of the incorruptible God to the likeness of the image of a corruptible man and of birds and fourfooted beasts and serpents: for they were the people's guides or followers into all those idolatries, and served the creature more than the Creator, who is blessed for ever. But in this other the heavenly city, there is no wisdom of man, but only the piety that serves the true God, and expects a reward in the society of the holy angels and men, that God may be all in all.'

Book XV begins with the contrary course of the two cities in history. Cain built the first city; not Abel, who was always a pilgrim.

'It is recorded of Cain that he built the city, but Abel was a pilgrim and built none. For the city of the saints is above, though it have citizens here upon earth, wherein it lives as a pilgrim until the time of the kingdom come, and then it gathers all the citizens together in the resurrection of the body and gives them a kingdom to reign in with their king for ever and ever.'

Chapter 4 describes the earthly city. Peace is the aim of its life. This it can win only by war. Cain's effort is compared with the building of Rome by Romulus, who also slew his brother. Once more he compares them in regard to Seth and Enos.

In XV, 21 he sums it up:

'Thus the two cities are described to be seated, the one in worldly possession, the other in heavenly hopes, both coming out at the common gate of mortality, which was opened in Adam; out of whose condemned race, as out of a putrefied lump, God elected some vessels of mercy and some of wrath; giving due pains unto the one, and undue grace unto the other, that the citizens of God upon earth may take this lesson from the vessels of wrath, never to rely on their own election, but

13

hope to call upon the name of the Lord: because the natural will which God made (but yet here the Unchangeable made it not changeless) may both decline from Him that is good and from all good to do evil, and that by freedom of will: and from evil also to do good, but that not without God's assistance.'

Book XVI goes on with the history. Augustine condemns in parentheses the idea of inhabitants at the Antipodes. The supreme type of the earthly city is the Tower of Babel. The course continues until the second period, that of Abraham, and the third, that of the Mosaic Law. From now onwards the city of God becomes represented for practical purposes by the Hebrew nation. Therefore it takes on some of the qualities of an earthly State. This gives occasion to S. Augustine to argue that all the promises of permanence in the Old Testament could not refer to the Jewish State but must have their fulfilment in that city eternal in the heavens. This is true in especial of all the promises to David (XVII, 16). He is led to argue that peace is no enduring condition on earth, but belongs of right only to the life beyond.

In Book XVIII we get to the course of the *civitas terrena, i.e.* the whole topic of Vico. That is represented in the Assyrian monarchy; but certain criticisms of Grecian myths and Egypt occur. We may cite here the vivid words of Vives on the following chapters:

'In this eighteenth book we were to pass many dark ways and oftentimes to feel for our passage, daring not fix one foot until we first groped where to place it, as one must do in dark and dangerous places. Here we cannot tarry all day at Rome, but must abroad into the world's farthest corner, into lineages long since lost, and countries worn quite out of memory; pedigrees long ago laid in the depth of oblivion must we fetch out into the light like Cerberus, and spread them openly. We must into Assyria, that old monarchy scarcely once named by the Greeks; and Sycionia, which the very princes thereof sought to suppress from memory themselves, debarring their very fathers from having their names set on their tombs, as Pausanias relateth; and thence to Argos, which being held the most antique state of Greece is all enfolded in fables; then Athens, whose nimble wits

14

aiming all at their country's honour, have left truth sick at the heart, they have so cloyed it with eloquence and wrapped it up in cloudes. Nor is Augustine content with this, but here and there casteth in hard walnuts and almonds for us to crack, which puts us to shrewd trouble ere we can get out the kernel of truth, their shells are so thick. And then cometh the Latin gests, all hacked in pieces by the discord of authors. And thence to the Romans; nor are the Greek wise men omitted. It is fruitless to complain lest some should think I do it causeless. And here and there the Hebrew, runneth like veins in the body, to show the full course of the Two Cities, the Heavenly and the Earthly. If any one travelling through those countries and learning his way of the cunningest should for all that miss his way sometimes, is not he pardonable? If any pass through, will anyone think him less diligent in his travel? None, I think. What then if chance or ignorance lead me astray out of the sight of divers mean villages that I should have gone by, my way lying through deserts and untracked woods and seldom, or never, finding any to ask the right way of. Am I not to be borne with? I hope yes. Varro's Antiquities are all lost; and the life of Rome. None but Eusebius helped me in Assyria, but that Diodorus Siculus and some others set me in once or twice.

I had a book by me called Berosus by the booksellers, and somewhat I had of Joannes Annius, goodly matters truly, able to fright away the reader at first sight. But I let them lie still; I love not to suck the dregs or fetch fables out of frivolous pamphlets, the very rackets wherewith Greece bandieth ignorant heads about. Had this work been a child of Berosus I had used it willingly; but it looketh like a bastard of a Greek sire. . . . If any man like such stuff, much good may it do him. I will be none of his rival. . . . Concerning Athens, Rome, Argos, Latium, and the other fabulous subjects, the reader hath heard whatsoever my diversity of reading affordeth, and much from the most curious students therein that I could be acquainted withall. He that liketh not this thing, may find another, by and by, that will please his palate better, unless he be so proudly testy that he would have these my pains for the public good, of power to satisfy him only. The rest, the Commentaries themselves will tell you' (On *De Civitate*, XVIII, i.)

Prophecy comes in and the conflicts of philosophers. The rise and early progress of Christianity are now described. The *Civitas Dei* is beginning to be identified with the Church; but Augustine emphasises the uncertainty of its true membership owing to the scarcity of the elect. The book thus concludes the history on earth:

'Now it is time to set an end to this book, wherein, as far as need was, we have run along with the courses of the two cities in their confused progress, the one of which, the Babylon of the earth, has made her false gods of mortal men, serving them and sacrificing to them as she thought good; but the other, the heavenly Jerusalem, she has stuck to the only and true God, and is his true and pure sacrifice herself. But both of these do feel one touch of good and evil fortune, but not with one faith, nor one hope, nor one law: and at length at the last judgment they shall be severed for ever, and either shall receive the endless reward of their works. Of these two ends we are now to discourse.'

Book XIX proceeds to the discussion with which we began, the thought of the *summum bonum*. Augustine says that this can be found only in the world beyond. After admitting that society is integral to human life, he points to some of its inevitable miseries on earth—war, insecurity—and becomes eloquenton the value of peace.

(C 11.) 'We may therefore say that peace is our final good, as we said of life eternal. Because the Psalm says unto that city, whereof we write this laborious work: "Praise the Lord, O Jerusalem, praise thy Lord, O Sion; for He hath made fast the bars of thy gates and blessed thy children within thee; He giveth peace in thy borders." When the bars of the gates are fast, as none can come in, so none can go out. And therefore this peace which we call final is the borders and bounds of this city; for the mystical name hereof, Jerusalem, signifies a vision of peace. But because the name of peace is ordinary in this world where eternity is not resident, therefore we choose rather to call the bound, wherein the chief good of this city lies, "life eternal." . . . The good of peace is generally the greatest wish of the world, and the most welcome when it comes. Whereof I

16

think one may take leave of our reader, to have a word or two more, both because of the city's end, whereof we now speak, and of the sweetness of peace, which all men do love.'

(C. 12.) 'Who will not confess this with me, who marks man's affairs and the general form of nature? For joy and peace are desired alike of all men. The warrior would but conquer; war's aim is nothing but glorious peace. What is victory but a suppression of resistants; which being done, peace follows? So that peace is war's purpose, the scope of all military discipline and the limit at which all just contentions level. All men seek peace by war, but none seek war by peace. For they that perturb the peace they live in, do it not for hate of it, but to show their power in alteration of it. They would not disannul it, but they would have it as they like; and though they break into seditions from the rest, yet must they hold a peaceful force with their fellows that are engaged with them, or else they shall never effect what they intend. Even the thieves themselves, that molest all the world besides them, are at peace amongst themselves. . .

'What tiger is there that does not purr over her young ones and fawn upon them in her tenderness? What kite is there, though he fly solitarily about for his prey, but will seek his female, build his nest, sit his eggs, feed his young, and assist his mate in her motherly duty, all that in him lies? Far stronger are the bands that bind man unto society, and peace with all that are peaceable; the worst men of all do fight for their fellows' quietness and would (if it lay in their power) reduce all into a distinct form of state drawn by themselves, whereof they would be the heads, which could never be, but by a coherence either through fear or love. For herein is perverse pride an imitator of the goodness of God having equality of others with itself under Him, and laying a yoke of obedience upon its fellows, under itself instead of Him; thus hates it the just peace of God, and builds an unjust one for itself. Yet can it not but love peace, for no vice however unnatural can pull nature up by the roots. . . .'

(C. 13.) 'The body's peace therefore is an orderly disposal of the parts thereof; the unreasonable soul's, a good temperature of the appetites thereof; the reasonable soul's, a true harmony

17

between the knowledge and the performance. That of body and soul alike, a temperate and undiseased habit of nature in the whole creature. The peace of mortal man with immortal God is an orderly obedience unto his eternal law, performed in faith. Peace of man and man is a mutual concord; peace of a family, an orderly rule and subjection amongst the parts thereof; peace of a city, an orderly command and obedience amongst the citizens; peace of God's City, a most orderly coherence in God and fruition of God; peace of all things is a well disposed order. . . .'

(C. 14.) 'All temporal things are referred unto the benefit of the peace which is resident in the terrestrial city, by the members thereof; and unto the use of the eternal peace by the citizens of the heavenly society. . . .'

'Now God, our good Master, teaching us in the two great commandments the love of Him, and the love of our neighbour, to love three things, God, our neighbours and ourselves, and seeing he that loves God offends not in loving himself—it follows that he ought to counsel his neighbours to love God and to provide for him in the love of God, sure he is commanded to love him as his own self. So must he do for his wife, children, family and all men besides, and wish likewise that his neighbour would do as much for him, in his need; thus shall he be settled in peace and orderly concord with all the world. The order whereof is, first, to do no man hurt, and, secondly, to help all that he can. So that his own have the first place in his care and those his place and order in human society affords him more conveniency to benefit. Whereupon S. Paul says: "He that provideth not for his own and, namely, for them that be of his household, denieth the faith and is worse than an infidel." For this is the foundation of domestic peace, which is an orderly rule and subjection in the parts of the family, wherein the provisors are the commanders, as the husband over his wife, parents over their children, and masters over their servants; and they that are provided for obey, as the wives do their husbands, children their parents, and servants their masters. But in the family of the faithful man, the heavenly pilgrim, there the commanders are indeed the servants of those they

18

seem to command; ruling not in ambition, but being bound by careful duty; not in proud sovereignty but in nourishing pity.'

(C. 15.) 'Thus has nature's order prevailed and man by God was thus created.' But sin ruled all. 'Sin is the mother of servitude and the first cause of man's subjection to man.' Dominion in the strict sense existed only between man and dumb animals. Yet for all that obedience is our duty; and the family is ever a part of the city.

In Chapter 17 we find the two ends described; one is earthly peace alone, the other has its other-worldly reference. Yet this heavenly city has members in all earthly cities, gives them true peace and the heavenly hope. Augustine goes on discussing (Chapter 21) Cicero's definition of a republic in which justice is an integral element. On that hypothesis Rome never was a commonwealth, since justice cannot be where the true God is not worshipped. But in Chapter 24 he gives another definition under which any stable state can be grouped. No true virtue exists apart from God, yet earthly peace is needed and must be used by the citizens of the heavenly state.

Book XX is concerned with the Last Judgment. In Chapter 6 Augustine argues that the first resurrection has already taken place in the conversion of sinners to Christ. The millennial kingdom is not, as the Chiliasts say, a future reign of Christ in the world, but is the present kingdom of the Church. This is the binding of the devil. It began with the spread of the Church outside of Judaism. The 'thrones and they that sat upon them' are the rulers of the Churches. The souls that reign with Christ a thousand years are the martyrs. The beast is the society of wicked man, opposed to the company of God's servants and fighting against His holy city. This society consists not only of open enemies but also of tares among the wheat. More apologetic discussion concludes the book.

Book XXI is concerned with the pains of the lost. We have an interesting passage on the miseries of life.

The last Book XXII gives an account of the felicity of the saved and the eternal bliss of the kingdom of God. Here apologetic follows concerning the Incarnation and the miraculous, in order to refute contemporary errors. After a description of the ills of life comes an eloquent passage on the goods of human life. Those passages form an interesting contrast:

(C. 22.) 'Concerning man's first origin our present life (if such a miserable estate can be called a life) does sufficiently prove that all his children were condemned in him. What else does that horrid gulf of ignorance confirm, whence all error has birth, and wherein all the sons of Adam are so deeply drenched, that none can be freed without toil, fear and sorrow? What else does our love of vanities affirm, whence there arises such a tempest of cares, sorrows, repinings, fears, mad exultations, discords, altercations, wars, treasons, furies, hates, deceits, flatteries, thefts, rapines, perjuries, pride, ambition, envy, murder, parricide, cruelty, villainy, luxury, impudence, unchastity, fornications, adulteries, incests, several sorts of sins against nature (filthy even to be named), sacrilege, . . . false witnesses, false judgments, violence, robberies, and suchlike, out of my remembrance to reckon, but not excluded from the life of man? All these evils are belonging to man and arise out of the root of that error and perverse affection which every son of Adam brings into the world with him.'

Augustine points out that the discipline of children has no other meaning. 'What is the end of all these but to abolish ignorance and to bridle corruption both which we come wrapped into the world withal.' He goes on:

'To omit the pains that enforce children to learn the (scarcely useful) books that please their parents, how huge a band of pains attend the firmer state of man and be not peculiarly inflicted on the wicked, but generally impendent over us all, through our common estate in misery! Who can recount them, who can conceive them? What fears, what calamities does the loss of children, of goods or of credit, the false dealing of others, false suspicion, open violence and all other mischiefs inflicted by others, heap upon the heart of man? Being generally accompanied with poverty, imprisonment, bands, punishments, tortures, loss of limbs or senses, prostitution to beastly lust, and other such horrid events? So are we afflicted on the other side with chances *ab externo,* with cold, heat, storms, showers, deluges, lightnings, thunder, earthquakes, falls of houses, fury of beasts, poisons of airs, waters, plants and beasts of a thousand sorts, stinging of serpents, biting of mad dogs, a strange accident wherein a beast most sociable and familiar with man shall sometimes become more to be feared than a lion or a dragon, infecting him whom he bites with such a furious madness, that he is to be feared by his family worse than any wild beast. What misery do navigators now and then endure? Or travellers by land? What man can walk anywhere free from sudden accidents? One coming home from the court (being sound enough on his feet) fell down, broke his leg and died of it; who would have thought this that had seen him sitting in the court? Eli, the priest, fell from his chair where he sat, and broke his neck. What fears are husbandmen, yea all men, subject unto, that the fruits should be hurt by the heavens or earth or caterpillars or locusts or such pernicious things! Yet when they have gathered them and laid them up they are secured. Notwithstanding I have known granaries full of corn borne quite away with an inundation.'

And so forth.

Augustine's tone may seem gloomy. But it must be borne in mind that the times were not bright. The reason of this book was the breaking up of the long centuries of Roman prosperity. As it neared its end, the storm burst even in Africa. Augustine's life was passed in a series of changes like those which divide the jubilees of Queen Victoria from the silver wedding of her grandson. It may indeed be argued that the habitual assumptions of Western civilisation both in Europe and America have been too optimistic ; that they assume peace and progress as natural and inevitable, and that the advance of physical science led to an altogether too favourable view of the reduction of pain in human life in a state of things rarely realised in history. It may be thought that the temper of Augustine, of the Middle Ages, and of the present, is more truly universal than that of the protected Roman Empire, of China, or of the Victorians. Anyhow we can parallel S. Augustine from writers in many ages, not only the Book of Job, but Richard Baxter, the author of a book curiously suggestive of the 'De

Civitate Dei'—'The Saints' Everlasting Rest.' In that incomparable style of the seventeenth century he declares:

(VII, 12.) 'Oh, the hourly dangers that we poor sinners here below walk in! Every sense is a snare, every member a snare, every creature a snare, every mercy a snare, and every duty a snare to us. We can scarce open our eyes but we are in danger; if we behold those above us, we are in danger of envy; if those below us, we are in danger of contempt; if we see sumptuous buildings, pleasant habitations, honour and riches, we are in danger to be drawn away with covetous desires; if the rags and beggary of others, we are in danger of self-applauding thoughts and unmercifulness. If we see beauty it is a bait to lust; if deformity, to loathing and disdain.'

(VII, 15.) 'The Church on earth is a mere hospital; which way ever we go we hear complaining; and into what corner soever we cast our eyes we behold objects of pity and grief; some groaning under a dark understanding, some under a senseless heart, some languishing under unfruitful weakness, and some bleeding for miscarriages and wilfulness, and some in such a lethargy that they are past complaining; some crying out of their pining poverty; some groaning under pains and infirmities; and some bewailing a whole catalogue of calamities, especially in days of common sufferings when nothing appears to our sight but ruin; families ruined; congregations ruined; sumptuous structures ruined; cities ruined; country ruined; court ruined; kingdom ruined; who weeps not, when all these bleed?'

(VII, 16.) 'Oh, the dying life that we now live; as full of suffering as of days and hours! We are the carcasses that all calamities prey upon; as various as they are, each one will have a snatch at us, and be sure to devour a morsel of our comfort. . . . As all our senses are the inlets of sin, so they are become the inlets of our sorrow. Grief creeps in at our eyes, at our ears, and almost everywhere; it seizes upon our heads, our hearts, our flesh, our spirits, and what part doth escape it? Fears do devour us and darken our delights, as the frosts do nip the tender buds: cares do consume us and feed upon our spirits, as the scorching sun doth wither the delicate flowers. Or, if any saint or stoic have

22

fortified his inwards against these, yet is he naked still without; and if he be wiser than to create his own sorrows, yet shall he be sure to feel his share, he shall produce them as the meritorious, if not as the efficient, cause. What tender pieces are these dusty bodies! What brittle glasses do we bear about us; and how many thousand dangers are they hurried through; and how hardly cured, if once cracked! Oh, the multitudes of slender veins, of tender membranes, nerves, fibres, muscles, arteries, and all subject to obstruc-tions, exesions, tensions, contractions, resolutions, every one a fit subject for pain and fit to communicate that pain to the whole; what noble part is there that suffereth its pain or ruin alone?'

But Augustine does not stop at this. The Puritan ideal with its extreme of otherworldliness could see little good in the natural and relative. Not so Augustine. In Chapter 24 he almost outdoes his previously cited passage in his anxiety to show the reality of earthly goods—goods distinct from the life of grace.

'Besides the disciplines of good behaviour and the ways to eternal happiness (which are called virtues), and besides the grace of God which is in Jesus Christ, imparted only to the sons of the promise, man's invention has brought forth so many and such rare sciences and arts (partly necessary and partly voluntary), that the excellency of his capacity makes the rare goodness of his creation apparent, even then when he goes about things that are either superfluous or pernicious, and shows from what an excellent gift he has those his inventions and practices. What variety has man found out in buildings, attires, husbandry, navigations, sculpture, and imagery! What perfection has he shown in the shows of theatres, in taming, killing and catching wild beasts! What millions of inventions has he against others and for himself in poisons, arms, engines, stratagems and suchlike! What thousands of medicines for the health, of meats for the throat, of means and figures to persuade, of eloquent phrases to delight, of verses for pleasure, of musical inventions and instruments! How excellent inventions are geography, arithmetic, astrology and the rest! How large is the capacity of man, if we should stand upon particulars! Lastly, how cunningly and with what exquisite wit have the philosophers and the heretics defended their very errors, it is strange to imagine. For here we speak of the nature of man's soul in general, as man is mortal, without any reference to the way of truth whereby he comes to the life eternal.'

After dilating on the marvels of the human body, he goes on to natural beauty.

'And then for the beauty and use of other creatures, which God has set before the eyes of man (though as yet miserable and amongst miseries), what man is liable to recount them? The universal gracefulness of the heavens, the earth and the sea, the brightness of the light in the sun, moon and stars, the shades of the woods, the colours and smells of flowers, the numbers of birds and their varied hues and songs, the many forms of beasts and fishes whereof the least are the rarest (for the fabric of the bee or the ant is more to be wondered at than the whales), and the strange alterations in the colour of the sea (as being in several garments), now one green, then another, now blue, then purple? How pleasing a sight sometimes it is to see it rough, and how more pleasing when it is calm! And O what a hand is that, that gives so many meats to assuage hunger! So many tastes to those meats (without help of cook), and so many medicinal powers to those tastes! How delightful is the interchange of day and night! the temperateness of air and the works of nature in the barks of trees and skins of beasts! Oh, who can draw the particulars? How tedious should I be in every peculiar of these few that I have here as it were heaped together, if I should stay upon them one by one! Yet are all these but solaces of men's miseries, no way pertinent to his glories.

'What then are they that his bliss shall give him, if that his misery has such blessings as these? What will God give them whom He has predestinated unto life, having given such great things even to them whom He has predestinated unto death? What will He give them in His kingdom, for whom He sent His only Son to suffer all injuries even unto death upon earth? Whereupon S. Paul says unto them: "He who spared not His own Son, but gave Him for us all unto death, how shall He not with Him give us all things also?" When this promise is fulfilled,

O what shall we be then? How glorious shall the soul of man be without all stain and sin, that can either subdue or oppose it, or against which it need to contend: perfect in all virtue and enthroned in all perfection of peace!

How great, how delightful, how true shall our knowledge of all things be there, without all error, without all labour, where we shall drink at the spring-head of God's aspience, without all difficulty and in all felicity! How perfect shall our bodies be, being wholly subject unto their spirits, and thereby sufficiently quickened and nourished without any other sustenance, for they shall now be no more natural, but spiritual; they shall have the substance of flesh quite exempt from all fleshly corruption.'

In Chapter 25 he points out that 'as touching the good things of the mind which the blessed shall enjoy after this life, the philosophers and we are both of one mind. Our difference is concerning the resurrection,' which he proceeds to argue. Of Porphyry, who has on the whole his deepest reverence, of Plato and Varro, Augustine speaks here, as always, in terms of honour, almost love. In the last chapter he enlarges on the *visio pads* and the eternal felicity of the city of God. It is interesting as well as eloquent, for it brings out the human and non-abstract quality of Augustine's theology:

(C. 35.) 'How great shall that felicity be, where there shall be no evil thing, where no good thing shall lie hidden; there we shall have leisure to utter forth the praises of God, which shall be all things in all! For what other thing is done, where we shall not rest with any slothfulness, nor labour for any want, I know not. . . . What the motions of those bodies shall be there I dare not rashly define, when I am not able to dive into the depth of that mystery. Nevertheless both the motion and the state, as the form of them, shall be comely and decent, whatsoever it shall be, where there shall be nothing which shall not be comely. Truly, where the spirit will, there forthwith shall the body be; neither will the spirit will anything, which may not beseem the body nor the spirit. There shall be true glory, where no man shall be praised for error or flattery. . . . There is true peace, where no man suffers anything which may molest him, either from himself or from any other. He himself shall be the reward of virtue, which has given virtue, and has promised Himself unto him, than whom nothing can be better and greater. For what other thing is that which He has said by the Prophet: "I will be their God and they shall be My people": but I will be whereby they shall be satisfied. I will be whatsoever is lawfully desired of men, life, health, food, abundance, glory, honour, peace and all good things? For so also is that rightly understood which the Apostle says: "That God may be all in all." He shall be the end of our desires, who shall be seen without end, who shall be loved without any satiety and praised without any tediousness. . . . There we shall rest and see, we shall see and love, we shall love, and we shall praise. Behold what shall be in the end without end? For what other thing is our end but to come to that kingdom of which there is no end?

'I think I have discharged the debt of this great work by the help of God. Let them which think I have done too little and them which think I have done too much, grant me a favourable pardon. But let them not think I have performed enough, accepting it with a kind congratulation; give no thanks unto me but "unto the Lord with me." Amen.'

This brief outline makes this much clear. The 'De Civitate Dei' is apologetic and theological. It is not a treatise on polity, whether ecclesiastical or civil. All S. Augustine's philosophical reading has left traces— and every kind of dialectic is displayed. As apologetic it is more effective against paganism than against the Platonists. Too much is assumed in regard to Jewish and Christian history. The book might reassure those within the Church whose faith was shaken. It would hardly arrest those without. It has the interest and also the coruscating irrelevance that comes from a great variety of topics. The thread is there, but sometimes it is hard to disentangle. Compare this book with such a work of apology as that of Origen against Celsus. We note how much larger the Church looms in the view of S. Augustine. It is no set of propositions which he is defending in a dialectic debate with other philosophers; although he can do this and does it in detail. But it is a social life which he sets up against another form of social life. The treatment is less individualist than that of Origen—though the latter had to

26

follow the course taken by Celsus. First we may observe that what impressed Augustine was the witness of the vastness of the Church and its triumph. As he says in a sermon:

'What do we see which they saw not? The Church throughout all nations. What do we not see which they saw? Christ present in the flesh. As they saw Him and believed concerning the Body, so do we see the Body; let us believe concerning the Head. Let what we have respectively seen help us. The sight of Christ helped them to believe the future Church; the sight of the Church helps us to believe that Christ has risen. Their faith was made complete, and ours is made complete also. Their faith was made complete by the sight of the Head, ours is made complete from the sight of the Body.' (*Sermon* lxvi. (cxi.) § 6.)

Probably those are right who say that in this respect also—if in nothing else—Augustine is epoch-making, that all his apologetic rests on the idea of Church. This characteristic would be developed in the Donatist controversy. It must be admitted, however, that such a view of him is not universally held, and some would put the distinctive basis of S. Augustine in the idea not of the Church, but of grace.[4]

Secondly we note the aggressive tone of the book. Despite his references to Plato and his real debt to Plotinus and Porphyry, Augustine is far more intransigent than Clement of Alexandria, who would treat Christianity as but the coping-stone of Greek thought. It is not as a superior gnosis, but it is as a scheme of Redemption, that Augustine commends Christianity, and values it for himself. The cause of this lies partly in that doctrine of original sin which was so strongly held by Augustine, and even was in some degree being developed while this book was in process. It is the point of the whole book.

Another note is the stress laid on the ethical difference between Christianity and its competitors—though that is not a novel feature. Augustine knows that it is not speculative truth but conduct that shows the greatest difference. Also he is aware that he is dealing with a dying interest. Paganism was uttering its death-cry (for the time). Clear is his note of triumph in the conquering and universal power of the Church.

27

History including miracle plays a great part. The destruction of Jerusalem following the rejection of Jesus by the Jews is an emphatic evidence of the Gospel. The argument from miracles he states as many would state it now. A miracle is not contrary to nature but to what we know of nature. The argument depends on our conception of God. Augustine had no notion of the distinction between the natural—*i.e.* the physical —and the supernatural. Nature means the whole world of God's order—all that happens. The problem is whether God's Will be paramount. All this has been treated by Mr. Lacey in his earliest Pringle-Stewart Lectures, 'Nature, Miracle and Sin.'

Above all we must bear in mind that the whole course of created existence is seen by S. Augustine as a conflict between two societies. However little some may make use of the figure of *Civitas Dei*, they have no right to deny its implications as against a doctrine purely individualist. Sin in Adam has become the property of the race, it is needful to show redemption in the order of historical development. The apologetic rests on a philosophy of history.

Finally it is of and in the antique world that Augustine wrote. The notion of him as medieval in temperament may have some evidence, yet it must be understood with care. The atmosphere of the book is of the old world. It is before Gelasius with his doctrine of the two powers, before Justinian. Only a little over a century had passed since Diocletian's effort at exterminating the Church. Less than that divided S. Augustine from the reaction under Julian.

Notes to Lecture I

[1] Weinand, H., *Die Gottesidee der Grundzug der Weltanschauung des hi. Augustins,* 1910, in Ehrhard und Kirsch, *Forschungen,* X. ii. p. i. 'Wie die Geisteswerte der heidnischen Kulturwelt in ihm zusammenfliessen, so hat vom

fünften Jahrhundert ab die christliche Kulturwelt in ihm Wurzeln und Fasern. . . .

'Man hat darauf hinangewiesen, wie jede Neuerung bis herab auf den Socialismus unserer Tage, ihn zu dem Ihrigen zu machen sich bemüht.'

[2] E. Feuerlein, *Ueber die Stellung Augustins in der Kirchen- und Culturgeschichte* in Sybel's *Historische Zeitschrift.* Bd. 22, 1869, p. 300.

'Dieser Eine Mann mit dem brennenden und zur Ruhe gekommenen Herzen ist der Typus der mittelalterlichen Christenheit. Sein zügelloses und doch zuletzt gezügeltes Temperament repräsentirt jenen wilden Volksgeist, der mit der Völkerwanderung sich erhebt und seiner Zähmung durch die Kirche harrt, die ganze Hitze und Heftigkeit des Volksthums, das sich gleich ihm in der Versenkung ins Eine, Göttliche, in der religiösen Andacht abkühlen soll. Er der Sohn eines gebildeten Naturvolks, topographisch ausserhalb des Gebiets der neueuropäischen Menschheit gestellt, sollte den zu erwartenden Naturvölkern Weg und Steg ihrer ersten Cultur weisen dürfen.'

[3] H. Reuter, *Augustinische Studien,* p. 121 *n.* 'Das ganze Werk *De Civitate* bewegt sich auf dem scharf gefassten Gegensatz des Diesseits und Jenseits, der Gegenwart und der Zukunft als auf seiner Basis.'

[4] Reuter, *Augustinische Studien,* p. 45. ' Nicht indem er "Die Heilsbedeutung" der Kirche verteidigte ist er ein Neuerer geworden, sondern durch die Art, wie er diese nach Massgabe seines Begriffs der *gratia* erörtert.

'Nicht in dem Kirchenbegriffe ist die prinzipale Diff erenz zwischen dem System Augustin's und dem der Pelagianer zuhöchst zu suchen, sondern in dem Begriffe der Gnade.'

THE PHILOSOPHY OF HISTORY

HAD S. Augustine a philosophy of history? If so, what is it, and what is its value? These are the questions to which I seek the answer to-day. Here is a paragraph pertinent enough from Archdeacon Cunningham's Hulsean Lectures on 'S. Austin and his Place in the History of Christian Thought' (p. 114).

'He sets before us a philosophy of history—the continuous evolution of the Divine Purpose in human society: he contrasts the earthly polities which change and pass with the eternal City of God which is being manifested in the world: he shows how these two are intermingled, interacting now, but how different they are in their real nature: one is of the earth, centred only in earthly things, while the other, because it has its chief regard fixed on that which is Eternal, gives us the best rule for the things of time. The earthly city, which aimed only at earthly prosperity, failed to attain even that, while the Heavenly City, aiming at an Eternal Reality, supplies the best conditions for earthly good as well. It is in the hope of the final triumph of the City of God that the course of the world becomes intelligible, for then we may see that the rise and fall of earthly empires, the glories of ancient civilisation, the sufferings of men in their ruin, have not been unmeaning or in vain; for they have served to prepare for the coming of the kingdom of God.

'Thus it is that for S. Austin, faith in the Holy Catholic Church serves to render history intelligible. This faith was the key of knowledge, for it gave the first philosophy of history worthy the name. . .

'If we examine it more carefully even now we shall be amply rewarded. We may find new reasons to admire S Austin—the discrimination he occasionally displays in the use of evidence, the marvellous power of combining many isolated facts into a connected system, even though here and there he puts forward opinions which are hard to reconcile with his general position. But we may find greater merits than these: we may turn from the grandest modern account of the evolution of human progress—turn from Hegel himself—to St. Austin and feel that the historical system of the ancient father is more perfect and complete; inasmuch as he had a clearer conception of the beginning, and a more definite perception of the final end towards which the whole Creation moves.'

Stronger praise can be found. An Italian scholar, Professor Billed, wrote a book on Vico and S. Augustine. The object was to show that Augustine was the true originator in the field of the philosophy of history, that Vico but followed in his steps, although by some he is regarded as a pioneer. Dr. Reinkens in his inaugural address as Rector of the University of Breslau develops the theme of S. Augustine's philosophy of history in reference to modern life. He seeks to show that his system is an account of the progress of the world to a rational freedom. This is one side.[1]

Some modern interpreters of S. Augustine set little store by his philosophy of history. H. Schmidt declares that he reduces history to a nullity. Others speak as though the few remarks he made on the topic are not worth considering.[2] They point out how meagre is his picture of the course of the terrene state, how he overlooks almost all history, except Assyria and Rome—just glancing at Greece and Egypt. True, Augustine mentions the common interpretation of the four monarchies in Daniel, implying that the Church is the fifth. Still there is no consistent effort to take the student through the revolutions of human affairs, and to justify the ways of God to man in the rise and fall of kingdoms such, for instance, as we see in Bossuet's 'Discours sur l'histoire universelle.' To that we may retort that this discourse was implicit in the 'De Civitate Dei.'

What is certain is that S. Augustine was a man historically minded. He set out (he was compelled by the purpose of his apologetic) to be a spectator of all time and all created being. No

31

one who takes the Incarnation seriously can avoid some kind of philosophy of history. That event—if a fact—testifies at once to the importance of human life on earth, and shows its centre. Doubts of Christianity at this moment are largely due to the difficulty felt by many in making the events in Palestine the pivot of human history. The religion of the Incarnation cannot be mere theology— a system of notions developed from certain metaphysical propositions—nor can it be mere ethics, a code of laws on a theistic basis. It has to do with a life on earth, in which Christians hold that in the fulness of time— *i.e.* at the due moment in history—the eternal reality at the heart of things became self-revealed and self-limited in a living earthly person. The issue of this was the fulfilment of the Jewish theocracy in the Christian Church. Augustine moreover approached Christianity emphatically by way of the Church. No one who did that could ignore the problems which it involved. Take a definite historical fact as your centre, take an actual visible society as the special sphere of God's operation, a society which has a past and must have a future on earth; and then you are compelled to some philosophy of history. You cannot, like a sheer Platonist—and Augustine shows leanings that way—treat as of no account the whole development in time and space, as though this world were the dreams of the Absolute in a fit of absence of mind; and then it is the object of the enlightened by some mystical process to get away from those dreams into the reality of day, where there is no change, no growth and no personality. That was the ideal of many. Augustine at one time had it. At times, even as a Christian, he uses expressions which show how greatly Plato and Plotinus contributed to his mental composition. On the whole, his belief in the Church and his sense of immediate reality were too great. A man who does not give way to the temptation of a doctrinaire's system pure and simple, but has so much regard to the actual as S. Augustine, is bound to rest unsatisfied without some philosophy giving history a meaning. Nowadays many seem to think it will be all the same if we leave out the facts, content to breathe the atmosphere created by a former belief in them, and hold that the Christian has to do solely with certain principles.

If the facts of Christ's life on earth be treated as of little

32

account, Christian faith will become either a set of dogmatic propositions, metaphysically grounded, coupled with a not too well-grounded ethical code, inelastic and impracticable, or else a name for certain states of sentimental brooding or elation. Against this danger Augustine fought, as we do now. His sense of Christianity being embedded in fact governs his apologetic, and that despite his love of dialectic, and his acquaintance with current philosophy.

The Dean of Wells in his Commentary on the 'Epistle to the Ephesians' has shown how S. Paul saw in the Incarnation a philosophy of history. So did S. Athanasius.

S. Augustine does but draw this out. By the fifth century the Church had become a great human institution. It was not the preacher of an *Interims Ethik,* but an important part of the world historical process. That was true, whatever you thought about the Church. It was but natural that a mind like S. Augustine's, sensitive to every prevailing current, should try to look at all history as a great drama, of which the supreme crises are in Eden and Calvary. This much, however, we must concede at the outside to the minimisers. Augustine did not set out to compose a philosophy of history. His purpose was not to comprehend history, but to defend the Catholic Church. Even Hegel was moved by something more than a disinterested concern for the student who is trying to gather up the threads of fact. He wanted to show how his own philosophy of the Absolute could be brought into line with the development of mankind. History proved to Hegel an illustration of the doctrines of the Logic. Incidentally he wanted to justify the Prussian State, in which, as we know, with his lack of humour, he contrived to discern the self-presentation of the Absolute Idea.

However it may be with Hegel, the philosophy of history arose directly out of the method of Augustine's apologetic. It is not individualist. Augustine does not proceed on the method, too often deemed adequate, of taking separate points and arguing from them, in order to affect individual conversions. That is not his object. His purpose is this—to justify the Christians' God against the attacks made upon Him, to remove from the Church

33

the charge of having brought about the ruin of civilisation. Over against the shattered world-order, great in its ruin, he sets another order even greater. He shows that the security and justice and freedom, which pious Romans believed to be guaranteed by the Roman Empire, were not guaranteed, that they never could be guaranteed on earth, that they are a treasure not of the body but of the soul. 'Not dear city of Cecrops, but dear city of God,' the cry of the great Stoic Emperor, has the gist of the whole. The Stoic lived in independence of temporal vicissitude, without help from beyond. 'The Christian belongs to the city which hath foundations whose builder and maker is God.' 'I'm but a stranger here—Heaven is my home.' Over against Rome, the eternal city, Augustine puts Jerusalem the Golden. This he does not do *in abstracto*. He takes the two ideas incarnate in two societies. One modern commentator, Scholz, well describes the book as 'Faith and Unbelief, as shown in world-history.' Even if this be not a philosophy of history, strictly so called, it is at least a justification of the Church, historically conceived. This is evident in the opening paragraph. ('De Civitate,' I. 1.)

'That most glorious society and celestial city of God's faithful, which is partly seated in the course of these declining times, wherein "he that liveth by faith" is a pilgrim amongst the wicked; and partly in that solid estate of eternity, which as yet the other part doth patiently expect, until "righteousness be turned to judgment"; being then by the proper excellence to obtain the last victory, and be crowned in perfection of peace, have I undertaken to defend in this work: which I intend unto you (my dearest Marcellinus) as being your due by my promise, and exhibit it against all those that prefer their false gods before this city's founder. The work is great and difficult, but God the Master of all difficulties is our helper. For I know well what strong arguments are required to make the proud know the virtue of humility, by which (not being enhanced by human glory, but endowed with divine grace) it surmounts all earthly loftiness, which totters through the one transitory instability. For the King, the builder of this city, whereof we are now to discourse, hath opened his mind to his people in the Divine Law thus: "God resisteth the proud, and giveth grace to the humble." Now this which is indeed only God's, the swelling

34

pride of an ambitious mind affecteth also, and loves to hear this as parcel of his praise.

"Parcere subjectis, et debellare superbos."

"To spare the lowly, and strike down the proud."

Wherefore touching the temporal city (which longing after domination, though it hold all the other nations under it, yet in itself is overruled by the one lust after sovereignty) We may not omit to speak whatsoever the quality of our proposed subject shall require or permit.'

These two cities and societies are vague enough, and ill-defined in thought and imagination. Still, however much or little Augustine meant by contemplating all created history as the conflict of two opposed societies, he meant more than some writers such as Reuter and Troeltsch would seem to admit. Clearly, this scheme affords a framework under which the whole of history can be subsumed. You may say that the plan is imperfectly executed. Many people have thought that even of Hegel's explicit 'Philosophy of History.' It did not require the late war to make it seem an odd performance to try and classify all history as a progress towards freedom, and to find that freedom for ever embodied in the Prussian Absolutism.

Faults of construction we may admit. The picture of the two cities was vague. At times Augustine forgets all about it. It seems strange that after stating his object he should go off into an elaborate attack on the morals of popular idolatry. Yet when we think it out, we can see some relevance to the main theme. Augustine would, I suppose, have agreed that these earlier books demonstrate the inadequacy of the *Civitas terrena* as an ideal. Still it is well to be warned. The reader must put up with a great deal of irrelevance and with the amplification of all sorts of things which have no obvious bearing on the main point. The passage from Vives cited in the last lecture illustrates this.

Two presuppositions of any philosophy of history are in the mind of S. Augustine throughout. (1) The unity of the human race, involving, as its corollary, the doctrine of (2) the essential

35

sociability of man. The *Civitas Dei,he* says, can mean nothing less than the social life of the children of God. That one principle alone, according to Scholz, is a contribution of high value to world-history. [3] Even better than Aristotle did S. Augustine understand that true history begins only with a form of society. Also he emphasises the unity of the human race which is derived by its descent from Adam. This idea lies behind his doctrine of original sin.

The strong sense of providential government of the world which Augustine shares with Vico may be thought to be also essential to the philosophy of history. This view, however, may be doubted.[4] One who was an atheist or a pure agnostic, *e.g.* Comte, might still have a philosophy of history, provided that he held the two maxims stated above, without any reference to God.

Augustine's conception, which was avowedly derived from the Republic of Plato, that you can best judge of a nation by the analogy of an individual, helped him in some ways. In other it was a drawback. Alike in Plato and S. Augustine such a view may lead to a conception of morals which permits the extremities of persecution. All evil clericalism goes back to Plato.

The 'De Civitate Dei' then is sketchy and incomplete. If we are to justify it as a philosophy of history, in spite of this, we must go further. Augustine's philosophy of history is a philosophy of the time-process as a whole. That is why he is able—as Scholz (p. 138) complains— to treat world-history as an episode. History according to S. Augustine is not merely terrestrial. It is the whole course of social happenings in time, in relation to a timeless Deity. No one could be more profoundly imbued than was S. Augustine with the doctrine of the timeless reality of God. On that ground he felt the more need of relating this to the world of successive events. Hence his book involves a philosophy of creation and a theodicy, no less than an account of the 'education of the human race.' It is history, as a whole, history from the creation of light until the Last Judgment, that is the justification of God. Only on that tremendous canvas can he paint a picture that shall outmatch the gloomy Velasquezlike portrait of the world as set up for men's imagination by the sack of Rome. On this view much that seems at first sight irrelevant falls into place. Augustine begins, he must begin, with the Creation. The universe was not created in Time. Time and the world are coeval. They are the chosen achievement of God—the divine symphony which not even sin can rob of its beauty.

> 'God Himself is the best poet
> And the real is His song.'

Augustine's strong æsthetic tendency, his worship of beauty, comes out in the doctrine that history is in truth a heavenly song—that, in some way or other, the evil in it is overruled by the beauty of the whole— just as discords are resolved by a skilful composer

'Why rushed the discords in, but that harmony might be prized,' Augustine says in his interesting letter to Marcellinus ('Epist.,' 138):

'God is the unchangeable Governor as He is the unchangeable Creator of mutable things, ordering all events in His providence until the beauty of the completed course of time, the component parts of which are the dispensations adapted to each successive age, shall be finished, like the grand melody of some ineffably rare master of song.'

He lifts creation, before the beginning of earth; the first important event, the true beginning of the two societies, is the sin of Satan. The pride of Lucifer typifies all evil doing; it began among the angels that dichotomy into the two societies which is to last for ever, and as its counterpart set moving the course of redemption.

Augustine seems to have held the view that men are created to fill the gaps in the celestial choir caused by the exclusion of the fallen angels; that the elect are to fill up that number and no more. The devil's first sin was an act of freedom of will like that of Adam. God did not cause it, for evil is negative. It cannot be created. It is the choice of the lower, instead of fidelity to the essential nature of a spiritual being. The nature of all things, even of the devil, is good. It is the will, not the nature, that goes wrong.

We need not follow S. Augustine into the account of the Fall. It is familiar enough. Once more must be emphasised the immense import, in regard to the philosophy of history, of S. Augustine's strong doctrine of original sin. He can compare the whole course of human history to a single individual, and can parallel their several stages. It is true that the comparison is vague; he gives different classifications in different places. In the 'De Catechizandis Rudibus' there are six. Freedom for the race, which was all enclosed in the loins of Adam, was lost in the strict sense by the Fall. Men still have a choice, but only between different kinds of sinful acts. Some are worse than others and will meet with worse torments. Manifold is the hierarchy of hell. With the Fall begins the human part of the *Civitas tenena.* Yet the coming redemption always holds some. The two societies not only now, but in all ages, have been intermingled. The heavenly city goes back through Shem to Seth; the earthly to Cain. The Hebrew development is treated as the main embodiment of the *Civitas Dei.* The *Civitas tenena* develops through Assyria and Rome, though I am not sure that Augustine ever absolutely identifies even the old Roman Empire with the *Civitas tenena.*

The *Civitas Dei* began long ago; but in its fulness it came with the spread of the Gospel. There will be a mystical thousand years of the reign of Christ. This is to be followed by the bitterest of all persecutions; and the devil will once again be loosed. After this the establishment of the final goal of the two cities is easy. The goal of the *Civitas Dei* is the *pax œterna,* and the *visio dei.*

Dr. Reinkens argued that the end which the citizens of the heavenly city will reach is true freedom. Hence he can parallel S. Augustine with Hegel, making them both teach that the history of the world is the record of the progress towards rational freedom. I cannot but think that Reinkens is here misled by the wish to make out a historical parallel. It is peace, not freedom, that is the goal. Augustine doubtless thought that freedom *(non posse peccare)* would only be reached hereafter and would be reached then. But that is not to the purpose. The sack of Rome had been the greatest dramatic violation of the *Pax Romana.* The sense of security had suffered a shock only to be likened to that which we feel now. As compensation for this lost earthly peace Augustine gives a new security—the peace that passes understanding. He does not promise a new earthly security under the aegis of the Church. On the contrary he agrees that neither religion nor piety can guarantee earthly security, although both are in the hands of God, who gives power, sometimes to the bad in order to teach humility to the good, and sometimes by way of reward to those relatively virtuous. The only genuine security must be that which is beyond the changes and chances of this mortal life. That is the 'saints' everlasting rest'—to be won in the heavenly Jerusalem, the happy home, when the triumph is eternal and warfare is accomplished. Save in figure it does not attach to that partial representative of the *Civitas Dei* which we see here and now in the Church Militant. That is no more free from perilous conjuncture than is the secular state.

Clearly the conception of redemption through the sacrifice of the Cross, made effective by a visible and sacramental Church, set over against the worldly society, affords some kind of philosophy of history. It runs as a thread through the whole complicated pattern of created being. This it could hardly do if religion were purely individual. The paramount significance of the Church, viewed as the depository and dispenser of grace, is of the essence of this historical philosophy. True, it may be argued, and has been argued, that the predestinarianism of S. Augustine makes the other way, and reduces all to individualism. Augustine is not always consistent. The two conceptions of the sacramental visible Church and the *communio sanctorum* cross one another in a way that is often perplexing. But this difficulty is not decisive. No one is secure of salvation by baptism or even by communion. But they are conditions *sine qua non.* Witness Augustine's views on the condition of unbaptised infants. One of his grounds of controversy with Julius of Eclanum was, that the latter was willing to except infants unbaptised from the full penalty—to assign them to a sort of lower court.

The sketch of world-history is the weakest thing in the book. All, however, goes to emphasise his main thesis. History is a unity. No one before or since taught more plainly the solidarity of man. That renegade Englishman, Houston Stewart Chamberlain, in a book once overpraised even in England, condemned all notions of humanity. He said that there was no human race, only races—and preached a new Teutonic Christianity. Now we see this in its first flush of hot-gospelling.' The Foundations of the Nineteenth Century' gives a reinterpretation in the interests of *Deutschland über Alles*. All is based on a doctrine of the fundamental inequality of races. It is the direct contrary of the doctrine of the 'De Civitate Dei' and Augustine's frequent assertions that *proximus homini est omnis homo.*

This unity of history is so set forth as to be a theodicy. Augustine thought that the doctrine of original sin, with its accompaniment of arbitrary election, could be reconciled with Divine Justice. All men are *ipso jure* damned. The few who are saved may rejoice. Those who suffer the last penalty have nothing of which to complain. They go where they naturally belong. Those who escape have no merit, not even a turning of the will, for that is the work of irresistible grace. Certainly this justification may not seem to us satisfactory. Later theories, especially that of Molina, went far away from this. But the point here is that Augustine gave a view of the whole and claimed to justify the ways of God to men.

Also, history is seen as the education of mankind. Augustine was the product of the university and an academic teacher. Strongly imbued as he was with his own sense of experience, he was hardly likely to undervalue the progressive education of mankind in the arts. So distinctly sociable a being could not really despise the social arts. Like all men he was tempted at times to think his own course worthless for what it left out. But that thought is hardly permanent. In the background of his consciousness he was always aware of the possession of culture. Still with his conversion to Christianity and even the earlier conversion to Platonism, the other-worldly doctrine creeps in. All the goods of human life have only a relative value. No earthly good has excellence save, and in so far, as it leads us on. The topic of world-flight is strong in S. Augustine in all his later writings. It is plausible to argue that of this book it is the main theme.

Can that be? Whether he liked it or not—and I rather think he did—Augustine must have known himself to be one of the best educated men of the day. Like a modern Etonian condemning the public schools, yet all the while conscious that they have made him a little different from those who were not there—this attitude, whether social or scientific or religious, has always in it an element of pose. The pessimistic view of all worldly activities is clear enough in the 'De Civitate Dei.' But it is counteracted by that other conception under which he views history as a work of art; in that sublime sense of human power and the beauty of things which was cited in the last lecture. Nobody who felt that, could treat the sights and sounds of earth, the outward beauty of things or even the course and revolutions of family and national life, as a thing of no account. A famous story of S. Bernard relates how he passed by the lake of Geneva and was unaware. S. Augustine has pictured for ever the scene at Ostia, in which took place the conversation with his mother, to which all the ten books of the 'Confessions' are the prologue.

Scholz argues that Augustine's theory of predestination takes all meaning out of history; since everything is preknown, how can there be any real development? Augustine is aware of this difficulty and tries to meet it. [It is, by the way, a difficulty not confined to this doctrine, but to any view which gives history as a whole a meaning. If the world moves to a predetermined end, the real end is in the beginning and it is only an unwinding of a clock.] In the argument against Fatalism Augustine tries to meet this. He denies that the Divine fore-knowledge does away with freedom. Here he was right. Whether the same can be said of the effects of his doctrine of irresistible grace is another matter. It must be conceded that, to S. Augustine, history is the sphere of the revelation under transitory and earthly symbols of the Eternal and Changeless Being. All changes, individual and social, are guided to their appointed end by a Providence, which though infinitely patient is also infinitely powerful. That does not eviscerate history of meaning. Any teleological view of human life is open to the same objection. Augustine's view of the way in which grace changes the human will may or may not be tenable, but it is not determinist. Besides, not only does Augustine make God free. Calvin did that. He makes man free by nature. He never taught that the first sin of Adam was predetermined, or that of Satan. Luther and Calvin did. Moral evil came into the world by the wrong use of a will free from the outset. That is the thesis which he is ever laying down against the Manichæan doctrine. After the one evil act the will is dominated by concupiscence, and that in every member of the race. All that it does has the nature of sin. But even then its acts are not necessitated; a man can choose between ambition and self-indulgence, between the pride of heroism and the meanness of cowardice. Even the doctrine of irresistible grace is not mere fatalism. It does not make world-history the blind working out of a formula—like the obedience of a curve to its equation. His emphasis on miracles, and the positive arguments which he gives for them, form an evidence of this. God's world will move to its end. That is certain. Yet it moves through the reality of concrete and actual persons and societies set in a world of time and space. History is a real, not a phenomenal thing. It is a drama, not a cinema show. He can appeal to history elsewhere (*Episi.* cxxxvii. 'Ad Volusianum') as serving in its order as an argument for the truth of the Gospel.

'What man might not be moved to faith in the doctrine of Christ by such a remarkable chain of events from the beginning and by the manner in which the epochs of the world are linked together, so that our faith in regard to present things is assisted by what happened in the past, and the record of earlier and ancient things is attested by later and more recent events.'

If we look before and after on this doctrine, we find certain other points to note. The doctrine of the two cities is not original. Indeed the Apocalypse of S. John might well have suggested it. It is almost certain that Augustine took it from Tyconius, the Donatist whom he respected so greatly. In the edition of the 'Rules of Tyconius' by Professor Burkitt we can read all about the two societies, the one of God and the other of the devil. [5]

42

To Tyconius also is due the interpretation of the millennial kingdom, as exhibited by the Church. Nor does Augustine state his doctrine for the first time in the 'De Civitate Dei.' We find it fairly well developed in the earlier treatise, 'De Catechizandis Rudibus,' and the division of human life into six ages. The main outline is all there. It was reserved for this work to treat it with a vast sweep of imaginative vision, so as to embrace all created existence and to found thereon an enduring apologetic.

Later on Otto of Freising attempted to write a history of the world on the framework laid down by S. Augustine, concluding in precisely the same way with the Last Things. More famous is the work of Bossuet. His 'Discours sur l'histoire universelle' is what it professes to be, an attempt to see history in the light of the Incarnation. He takes it down to Charlemagne and had intended to take it further. The book is not an adaptation of S. Augustine's work. It is primarily historical, just as the former is primarily apologetic. It is far more detailed and better constructed. But like that of S. Augustine, Bossuet's aim was partly practical, and he boasted of a conversation with du Gouet which enabled him to put the argument from the destruction of Jerusalem in a convincing way. Bossuet treats more satisfactorily the course both of profane and sacred history, ending with the establishment of the definitely Catholic Empire in the West. This book, one of its author's greatest, owes much to S. Augustine. M. Hardy wrote a volume, showing how close was this dependence. That is in some degree true of all Bossuet's work. Even Jansenism was hardly more deeply soaked in S. Augustine than was Bossuet, who rarely preaches a sermon without an allusion to him.

Vice's 'Nuova Scienzia' proves a problem. What was the influence of the ' De Civitate Dei' in this— one of the most original and epoch-making books of modern times? Dr. Billeri in 'Giovanni-Battista Vico e S. Agostino' claims the mastery and originality all for S. Augustine, and boldly transfers to him any honour given to Vico. This treatment is extravagant. The purpose of the two writers is different. Augustine, it cannot be too often repeated, is an apologist. Vico is above all an enquirer. He wants to get a generalised scheme of historical development, and to destroy what may be called the academic superstition.

His attitude towards the earlier ages of classical history is curiously like that of Nietzsche. Above all he is anxious to rescue Homer from the imputation of being a teacher of philosophy and morals in the later sense, and to disabuse the reader of the notion that the virtues honoured in the heroic age were those of a settled and peaceful age, with the golden rule, at least in words, for its motto. He is anxious to show that the original development of men started from pure anarchism, with the patriarch ruling his family, as in the case of Polyphemus, through a ruthless aristocracy to a popular government and thence to monarchy (as, *e.g.* Rome), owing to the dissensions and unwillingness of men to work together and submit to law.

With a strong belief in original sin, he claims that God as the author of nature makes men's vices, lust, cruelty and ambition work together for good, so as to establish a stable and law-abiding society. This is a universal law all over the world. Feudalism in some form or other is the beginning of government, and monarchy comes at the close. Thus Vico is certainly at variance with writers like Filmer who treat monarchy as original, no less than he is with believers in democracy. It is a scheme entirely different from S. Augustine's —so different that at first sight one is disinclined to see any parallel. But we notice *(a)* his strong belief in the providential ordering of human affairs, *(b)* his making original sin the beginning of all profane history, *(c)* his reiterated assertion of the natural *sociability of man* as the eternal law of his being, *(d)* his repeated references to the 'De Civitate Dei' and his use of it, further, for his even more repeated use of ' Varro' (whose work we have not in the original). We may compare Vico's belief in Providence with S. Augustine's famous passage on the distribution of kingdoms. Only Vico goes more deeply, for he has the modern scientific spirit and its love of comparative method.

Augustine is mainly concerned with the Church, Vico with the world. It is hard to say how far Vico was prompted by S. Augustine or whether he intended consciously to counter his book. Probably the truer view is that S. Augustine appealed to him by the sweep of his thought and by his vision of world-history; but that, so far as the main idea is concerned,

44

Augustine ranked mainly as one writer among the many whom he cited. [6]

What Professor Flint says in his history of the ' Philosophy of History' is worth citing:

'It must have strongly confirmed Vico in some of his most fundamental convictions—in the belief of Providence in history, of order and law in human affairs, of particular passions and interests being rendered by supreme reason subservient to general ends, of the analogy of the growth of the individual to that of the race, of the futility of Epicurean chance and the Stoic fate, as principles of historical explanation. But his theory of history is by no means a simple continuation of that of Augustine; on the contrary, the differences between them are as profound as their resemblances. Vico does not, like Augustine, look upon history in relation to predestination, the fall, redemption, and the end of the world, but as a manifestation of human nature and of fixed laws. He conceives of Providence very distinctly from St. Augustine.'

Both the 'De Civitate Dei' and the 'Scienzia Nuova' are great books; both suffer from a good deal of bad arrangement. Both are things to be felt rather than learned. In different ways both have had enormous influence on thought. But one is not the child of the other. They are complementary, not contrary.

Notes to Lecture II

[1] Reinkens, *Die Geschichtsphilosophie des Heiligen Augustinus* (Schaffhausen, 1866), inaugural address as Rector of Breslau University, p. 36.

'Die ganze Verfassung und das ganze Gesetzbuch des himmlischen Staates ist in Einem Wort enthalten, und dies Wort heisst: *Freiheit*. Denn die Macht des freien Willens ist in dem Menschen dann wie bei den guten Engeln bis zu dem

Grade für das Gute in seiner göttlichen Rangordnung gesteigert, dass ihm eine Abweichung von der Ordnung der Liebe nicht mehr möglich ist, ebenso wenig wie ein Rückfall aus dem verklärten Zustand in den unverklärten. Ein Nöthigen in die Ordnung der Liebe durch äussere Gesetze und Befehle unter Androhung von Strafen ist undenkbar in dem Gottesstaate; in seinem ewigen Sabbate existirt auch der Begriff des knechtischen Dienstes nicht mehr. Gott selbst trägt die Krone; aber die Bürger des himmlischen Staates sind von Ihm mitgekrönt: sie herrschen mit Ihm, in dem sie Ihm huldigen, und da sie Ihm loben, empfangen sie Ehre, und die Geehrten erkennen ohne Ueberhebung, dass sie der Ehre würdig sind, und Niemand raubt und Niemand neidet sie ihnen. So wird es sein am Ende ohne Ende; denn welches andere Endziel hatten wir, als zu gelangen in das Reich ohne Ende?'

[2] H. Schmidt's two articles are to be found in the *Jahrbücher für Deutsche Theologie* (Gotha, 1861); *Des Augustinus Lehre von der Kirche,* vi. 197-255; and *Origenes und Augustin als Apologeten,* vii. 237-281 and viii. 261-325.

[3] H. Scholz, *Glaube und Unglaube in der Weltgeschichte,* p. 47. 'Wenn es richtig ist dass Geschichtsphilosophie und Soziologie zusammengehören, so ist Augustin der erste gewesen, der diesen Zusammenhang innerlich erfasst und wirksam ausgesprochen hat. Zwar hat schon Aristoteles den Menschen als ζῷον πολιτικόν gewürdigt, aber nur um den Staat daraus abzuleiten. . . Augustin hat den Fortschritt zur Geschichte gemacht, und die Möglichkeit des geschicht-lichen Lebens auf den geselligen Zusammenschluss der Individuen gegründet. Er hat erkannt, dass es Geschichte nur da gibt und dass Geschichte erst da beginnt, wo Menschen sind, die sich zu geordnetem Mit- und Aufeinander wirken verbinden. Er hat diesen Zusammenhang nicht nur geahnt, sondern deutlich ausgesprochen: unde Dei civitas . . . vel inchoaretur exortu vel progrederetur excursu vel adprehenderet debitos fines, si non esset socialis vita sanctorum? (xix. 5). Es ist nicht zuviel, wenn mann behauptet, dass Augustin sich durch diesen einen Satz ein bleibendes Verdienst um die Philosophic der Geschichte erworben hat; denn solange es eine Philosophic der Geschichte

gibt, wird sie mit diesem Satz beginnen und insofern immer auf Augustin als ihren geistigen Vater zurückblicken dürfen.'

[4] *Cf.* the following passages. There are many more:

(a) De Civ. Dei, v. i.—' Divina providentia regna constituuntur humana.'

(b) Ibid. v. ii.—' Sed nee exigui et contemptibilis animantis viscera, nee avis pennulam, nee herbae flosculum, nee arboris folium sine suarum partium convenientia et quadam veluti pace dereliquit; nullo modo est credendus regna hominum, eorumque dominationes et servitutes a suis providentiae legibus alienas esse voluisse.'

(c) Ibid. iv. 33.—' Deus igitur ille felicitatis auctor et dator, quia solus est verus Deus, ipse dat regna terrena et bonis et malis. Neque hoc temere et quasi fortuitu, quia Deus est, non fortuna, sed pro rerum ordine ac temporum occulto nobis, notissimo sibi, cui tamen ordini temporum non subditus servit, sed eum ipse tanquam dominus regit moderatorque disponit. Felicitatem vero non dat nisi bonis. Hanc enim possunt et non habere et habere servientes, possunt et non habere et habere regnantes ; quae tamen plena in ea vita erit, ubi nemo jam serviet. Et ideo regna terrena et bonis ab illo dantur et malis ne eius cultores adhuc in provectu animi parvuli haec ab eo munera quasi magnum aliquid concupiscant. Et hoc est sacramentum Veteris Testamenti, ubi occultum erat novum, quod illic promissa et dona terrena sunt, intelligentibus et tune spiritalibus quamvis nondum in manifestatione praedicantibus, et quae illis temporalibus rebus significaretur aeternitas, et in quibus Dei donis esset vera felicitas.'

[5] *The Rules of Tyconius,* edited by F. C. Burkitt. This should be read to see how close is the parallel. Augustine knew this book and made a lengthy summary of it in the third book of *De Doctrina Christiana.* Scholz, *Glaube und Unglaube in der Weltgeschichte,* has much in detail about the dependence of S. Augustine on Tyconius. The topic has been worked out by Hahn, *Tyconius Studien,* in Bonwetsch und Seeberg, *Studien;* see vi. 2, also Haussleiter, *Prot. Real-Encyclopädie,* xx. 851-5.

[6] Nourisson, *Philosophie de S. Augustin,* ii. 173. 'Sa conception d'une républic éternelle et naturelle, la meilleure possible dans chacune de ses espéces et ordonnée par la Providence divine, n'est qu'une application ou une transformation savante de l'idée mère de la Cité de Dieu.'

THE STATE

IN trying to comprehend S. Augustine's thought about the State, we must avoid one error, that of translating *Civitas* by State.[1] His thought, as I said, is eminently social. He thinks of good and bad as gathered into two societies. Only at the last judgment will the *Civitas terrena* be dissolved into its constituent atoms. But *civitas* is not for Augustine a term convertible with *respublica* ; and the *Civitas Dei* is to be found long before a visible Church existed, even before the call of Abraham. He speaks of the good and the evil as mystically two cities, stressing the word mystical. More than once he explains *civitas* as equivalent to society. The primary distinction is always between two societies, the body of the *reprobate* and the *communio sanctorum*; not between Church and State. With his strong doctrine of election, it is natural that he should follow Tyconius in his views of the *bipartite* nature of the body of God, *i.e.* The elect and the mererly nominal members. On earth these two bodies are intermingled, and always will be. Only partially and for certain purposes is the *Civitas terrena* represented by any earthly polity. The Church represents the *Civitas Dei* rather by symbol than by identification. This error is often made. Some phrases seem to point that way. But first of all the distinction is to be drawn as I have stated. Error has arisen by identifying *sans phrase* the *Civitas terrena* with the State as such; and by taking every predicate applied to the *Civitas Dei* as obviously intended for the Church Militant. It would be less inaccurate to represent it, in the familiar phrase, as the conflict between the Church and the World. Yet even this would not be right. The real divisison is one which will be made manifest at the Last Judgment, and not until then. All early distinctions are but the symbols, never adequate, of the final grouping into sheep and goats. Members of either body are found, and always will be found, in the terrene representative of the other. It is the superiority of other-worldly interests to those of this world which is the gist of all.

Hermann Reuter[2] goes on to remark that, even if we were using political terms to translate *civitas*, we ought to use the word 'city' rather than 'state.' That is true. Hardly is it of capital importance, since the antique conception of a commonwealth was derived from the city-state. I doubt if we gain much by saying that Cain was the founder of *a* city, not *the* State. What we have to try and grasp is what Augustine thought about the State; not what he thought about some States. Does he condemn the *Respublica?*

In his deduction of the two cities Augustine uses strong words on the effects of the lust of dominion. To Augustine it was, as to Nietzsche, 'the will to power' that is founded upon the direct opposite of neighbourly and Christian motives. Only he draws an opposite inference. The original relations of man to man are not without organisation. The family is primitve and divine, and an association of families is natural. The first kings were shepherds. Dominion, *i.e.* absolute despotic dominion in the sense of the Roman Law, the power of the *pater-familias,* of a master over slaves— that, as applied to man instead of animals, is due to sin. Those people who quarrel with this have no right to say that slavery is wrong now. Slavery owed its beginning to sin. None the less is it God's judgment—as a punishment—and must be borne.

In the earlier chapters of the Fourth Book Augustine decides on the whole against large Empires, though in one place he seems to admit that Rome acquired hers justly, on the ground of the iniquity of her enemies. But he takes the case of the first invader of the ancient hereditary monarchies, Ninus, as the classical instance of the foundation of an Empire obtained by force and fraud; and he decides that it is no better than a *grande latrocinium.* ('De Civitate,' IV. 6.)

'To war against one's neighbours and to proceed to the hurt of such as hurts not you, for greedy desire of rule and sovereignty, what is this but flat thievery, in a greater excess and quantity than ordinary?'

A page or two before he relates a story of Alexander the Great and the pirate, which is of a similar tenor.

Augustine's attitude in regard to slavery, and to private property in the sense of absolute dominion, is nothing new, although the lesson has not yet been learnt by the world. May it not be said that one of the things that men have been slowly learning is that rights of property are not absolute, and that they must give way to the public welfare? This sense of property, as of absolute *dominion*, has dominated modern Europe through the Roman Civil Law. Yet the other sense lies behind the Civil Law. It is the presupposition of Jurists like Ulpian and the Stoics. Their teaching pointed ultimately to the end of chattel slavery. It may point in the same direction in regard to extreme rights of private ownership. The moment you say that ownership is the creation of the law, you imply the power of revising it. The idea that something else, common ownership, is natural, and that legal division is conventional, runs throughout history. Augustine argues that the source of right must either be divine constitution or human. Since we hold our property by the law of the State, we must hold to the State's laws. He does not wish to upset them. This, he says, in reply to the Donatists, in a letter to Vincentius ('Epist.,' xciii. § 12):

'Since every earthly possession can be rightly retained only on the ground either of Divine Right, according to which all things belong to the righteous, or of human right, which is in the jurisdiction of the Kings of the Earth, you are mistaken in calling those things yours which you do not possess as righteous persons, and which you have forfeited by the laws of earthly sovereigns.'

According to Sommerlad,[3] Augustine set out to develop a theory of Church and State; but what as a fact he did was to 'lay down an industrial and economic programme for the Middle Ages.' I cannot think either of these statements to be well-grounded. The last thing that he set out to do was to give a theory of the relations of the Church and State. Most of the more important errors in the interpretation of the 'De Civitate' have their origin in this notion. With regard to the second point, in the 'De Opere Monachorum' he argues strongly for the need of manual labour in bodies of religious.[4] He will not have it that study and reciting the Divine Office are enough. That dictum may have helped to determine the character of Western monasticism. It may have inspired the Benedictine ideal. In so far, it helped to create an important element in mediæval civilisation. But it is surely a wild imagination to suggest that Augustine anywhere laid down a programme on socialistic lines for the Middle Ages; that that programme was for some centuries adopted, and was discarded at the Renaissance with the rise of modern capitalism.[5]

On the first point, Augustine said a great deal which has a bearing on Church and State as polities, and on their relations. Most of what he said could be used in more ways than one. In this and the following lecture I shall try to disentangle what he meant himself, and then in the last two to see what later times have made of the 'Civitas Dei.'

Once more let us recall the general aim of the book— an apology for the Church. That purpose does not cease with Book X. We can see this by the analysis of the last twelve books, how right down to the end he lays preponderant stress on the evidence for the faith in history and miracle.

Further, the Church which Augustine was defending was now in enjoyment not merely of peace, but of imperial patronage. The peace of the Church was a century old when he began the book. The era of Julian was over. The Council of Constantinople had achieved the victory of Catholicism in the Empire. Theodosius had stamped Christianity upon the legal system. Doubtless the penetration was not so deep as it became later in the work of Justinian. Still it was the one officially supported religion. Such was not the time for an intransigent history of the rights of the Church, or for a nullification of the State. The occasion itself of the book shows this. Augustine had to argue that the legal prohibition of sacrifice was not a calamity. Was it likely that at such a moment he would assert that the State was

52

a thing in essence evil? Yet that he is accused of doing. Ritschl, who followed Dorner, asserts that Augustine regarded civil government as such as being the organisation of sin.[6] Eicken, a very recent writer, says that with the peace of the Church, the Church showed itself more hostile to the State than in the days of persecution.[7] The Council of Nicea with its golden throne for the Emperor (as yet unbaptised) is an odd phenomenon, if that be so. But since this doctrine is set out in all earnestness by some of the most learned and acute minds, it must be rigidly examined before we are to reject it.

Can we then interpret the 'De Civitate Dei' as teaching that civil society is wrong in itself? Doubtless it teaches, as any Christian book would teach, that all earthly activities have their value only in the service of God. Human life, including the State, has no value save as a preparation. The 'heavenly home' is the goal. Few thoughtful Platonists wouls say less. If Augustine means no more than that earthly activities have a purely relative and provisional value, as compared with the enduring realities of the immortal life, we ought to beware of attributing to him any violently anti-political doctrine. The problem is no easy one. Augustine is too great to be always consistent. Still let us bear in mind this. Not only here but in his other works Augustine repeatedly quotes with approval the Apostolic injunctions about submission to the powers that be. He declares the Government of Nero to be God's ordinance, and goes out of his way to say so. He is emphatic on the duty of rendering to Caesar what belongs to him. He is always full of the glory of Rome, and is imbued with the value of social union and family life. Beyond all this he is opposed to the Donatists.

Reuter is right when he says that we cannot arrive at Augustine's political views—they never amount to a theory— from reading or studying the 'De Civitate Dei' by itself.[8] We must study the treatises written against the Donatists; also his letters and sermons and some of the minor works. Now it was the Donatists, not the Catholics, who adhered to the old Christian attitude of the days of persecution—that typified by the Apocalypse, in which is pictured a death struggle between the Imperial power and the Christian Church.[9] Yet in the Apocalypse we note that it is the Emperor as an object of worship that is condemned—never the idea of State authority. Much of S. Augustine's energies were occupied in combating the Donatists. Rather reluctantly he came to the conclusion that it was right to employ against them the forces of the civil government. He had thought differently in the days of his controversy with the Manichæans. Now that this policy won success, he gave rather reluctantly his adhesion to the views of his episcopal colleagues. Was it likely that, writing just after this, Augustine should turn round and condemn the State and all its works? It was the Donatists who claimed entire freedom from civil obligations. They were, in modern phrase, 'absolutists.' To them the State is an institution so profane as to be practically diabolical. That was the cry which Augustine had to meet. We can see how he met it in his reply to Petilian (II. 92). Petilian asks, 'What have you to do with kings who have never shown anything but envy to Christianity?' Augustine replies at length. The most important passage is in c. 210. In this he says that kings must serve God as kings:—for no man as a private individual could command that idols should be taken from the earth. But that when we take into consideration the social condition of the human race, we find that kings, in the very fact that they are kings, have a service which they can render to our Lord in a manner which is impossible for any who have not the power of kings. This is assuredly to admit the sacred office of a king as representative of the State.

There is another letter (*Ad Marcellinum*, 138, c. 15), one written to meet the charge of the pagans that Christianity was a civic peril, which affords even stronger evidence. After denying that Christianity condemns wars of every kind, he goes on:

'Let those who say that the doctrine of Christ is incompatible with the State's well-being, give us an army composed of soldiers such as the doctrine of Christ requires them to be; let them give us such subjects, such husbands and wives, such parents and children, such masters and servants, such kings, such judges—in fine, even such taxpayers and tax-gatherers— as the Christian religion has taught that men should be, and then let them dare to say that it is adverse to the State's well-being; yet rather let them no longer hesitate to confess that this doctrine, if it were obeyed, would be the salvation of every commonwealth.'

He points out that some form of State is needful to the worst tyrant and that the State is a natural and therefore a Divine necessity.

Still, there is evidence which tells the other way. First of all there is the main gist of the book—this is to depress the *Civitas terrena*. Of that there is no doubt; and if the *Civitas terrena* is to be identified with the civil State, as such, *cadit quaestio*. But the *Civitas terrena* is above all the society of the reprobate, a union largely unconscious and no less invisible than the invisible body of the elect. Only in so far as this society is represented by the State does it come in for condemnation. What is condemned is the World in Creighton's definition of it: 'human society organising itself apart from God.'

Then there is to be taken into account the remarkable passage, or couple of passages, in which Augustine condemns Imperialism (III. 10 and IV. 3, 15). At the most, however, this view only condemns great Empires. It does not depreciate, it rather exalts, the Commonwealth. Augustine sees how greatly the lust of power goes to the making of most great Empires. Rome he thinks had justice on its side. He dislikes the tyranny of strong nations over weak. He hazards the conjecture that the world would be most happily governed if it consisted, not of a few great aggregations secured by wars of conquest, with their accompaniments of despotism and tyrannic rule, but of a society of small States living together in amity, not transgressing each other's limits, unbroken by jealousies. In other words, he favoured a League of Nations—a condition, as he put it, in which there should be as many States in the world as there are families in a city. Still it is an organised State that he wants. There must be a union of families to create the city, and a union of associated governments, only no imperial power. Here is doctrine, not only social, but eminently political.

In another passage he contemplates a condition in which compulsion will not be needed. There will be no more necessity for it than in a well-governed family. It is always on the analogy

55

of the family that he thinks. But this is not to do away with law and government. Against the view that law is the expression of force; and no more, he sets out his doctrine that law has its true origin in consent.

On this point Vives makes a comment which is worth quoting (X. 4):

'Oh, what a few laws might serve man's life, how small a thing might serve to rule not a true Christian, but a true man. Indeed he is no true man that knoweth not and worshippeth not Christ. What serveth all these Digests, Codes, Glosses, Counsels and Cautels? In how few words doth our great Master show every man his due course. Love then Him which is above as well as thou canst, and that which is next thee like thyself, which doing thou keepest all the lawes and hast them perfect, which others attain with such toil, and scarcely keep with so many invitations and terrors. Thou shalt then be greater than Plato or Pythagoras with all their travels and numbers, than Aristotle with all his quirks and syllogisms.'

We may compare also a later passage of Vives on XIV. 28:

'With how excellent a breviate hath he drawn the great discourses of a good commonweal, namely that the rulers thereof do not compel or command, but, standing aloft like sentinels, only give warnings and counsels; thence were Rome's old magistrates called consuls, and that the subjects do not refuse or resist, but obey with alacrity.'

Most, however, turns on another argument— Augustine's discussion of Cicero's definition of a State, given in the 'De Republica.' Cicero there makes Scipio define a republic as *res populi. Populus*, however, must be explained. The words must be cited: '*Populum autem non omnem coetum multitudinis sed coetum juris consensu et utilitatis communione sociatum esse determinat*' (II. 21). In discussing this he fixes on the word *juris* and so makes justice to be of the essence of a State. This leads on to the famous tag *remota justitia quid regna nisi magna latrocinia*. But Augustine does not allow himself to be balked by this. He argues that there is some kind of commonwealth even

56

in a robber band.[10] They are bound by the social contract among themselves. There must be rules for the division of the spoil. In other words, there must be within them a relative and internal justice, even though in regard to the world at large they are outlaws. In other words, any association, if permanent, must have within it the nature of a State or part of it. He points out that Rome according to the description of Sallust had ceased to be a republic owing to the growth of corruption in morals. This would be true of many other States. (This argument is somewhat akin to the notion of Locke, that a State ceases *ipso facto,* if the principles of the original contracts are violated.)

Then later on (II. 21) he goes on to argue that if justice in the absolute sense be a *sine qua non* of a true commonwealth, then neither Rome nor any other pagan State was one. For you cannot have justice where the true God is not worshipped, and the only true commonwealth would be that wherein Christ is King.[11] In XIX. 20 and 21 he says much the same. If this were all, it might be held to be decisive, *i.e.* to prove that Augustine condemns the State, though he does not really make the Church a State even here. Even here I do not see that there would be anything more than religious toleration required for the condition to be fulfilled, *i.e.* the position would be that of the Roman Empire after the peace of the Church in the time of Constantine. Perhaps, however, Augustine's doctrine assimilating the State to an individual might be held by implication to preclude toleration.

Augustine does not stop here, although some of his interpreters, alike critics and disciples, have done so. He sees that either you must give the name State to Rome in all its changes, to the Greek republics and to the world-monarchies, or else you must find some other term that will enable you to classify them. Something must be wrong with Cicero's definition (or else with the Augustinian notion of justice) unless it can be applied to such societies as these. So he proceeds to give a definition of his own from which the word justice is excluded.[12]

'Populus est coetus multitudinis rationalis, rerum quae diligit concordi communione sociatus.'

This, he says, will include Rome, Babylon, or any other settled State. The really governing word here is *concordi*. It is some kind of consent and harmony that is necessary.[13] In an earlier passage he had adumbrated this, and said that this definition, as he would show, was *probabilior*. Augustine is like any modern who might argue, that the State, in the nature of things, is democratic, because democracy involves the recognition of human personality. That is a fact, which no legal system can make not to be a fact, merely by the process of denying it. You may lay down, for instance, that a slave is not a person, but a chattel, a thing. That does not make him one. He is a person. Your legal system is false to fact if it denies that. But the modern, who said that, would be unwise if he were to deny the name of State to governments which so acted. He could say if he liked that they were no true States. He could not say that they were not States. The moment you come to consider such a term as 'State,' you are tempted to put into its definition a description of its ideal form, so that a State comes to mean the perfect State. Thereupon, anything, that falls short of that, is outside the definition. According to Locke's definition, I believe that the English State must have disappeared with almost every parliament since 1832, because laws were passed interfering with the individualist basis. According to an opposite definition of sovereignty, that of Austin, it is at least plausible to say that there is no such thing, and never has been, as a true law in the United States of America.[*] Augustine's use of Cicero's definition, and his enlargement of the notion of justice so as to include true religion, must be treated in the same way.

That love to one's neighbour and to oneself (Augustine is no pure altruist), grounded on a love of God, are the greatest bonds of union among men must be the view of any Christian. So it is arguable that the Golden Rule is the foundation of political righteousness, and that the Golden Rule cannot be maintained apart from belief in God.

Meanwhile the world is very evil. So long as the heathen in his blindness bows down to wood and stone we must have a

58

number of communities that fall short of this ideal. They cannot be wholly without justice, or there would be no society at all, as Augustine most pertinently said even in regard to the robber bands. The good at which such societies aim—earthly peace and security—is a real good and no sham.[14] It is not to be despised or disturbed, but is to be used by the *Civitas Dei.* So far is it from being true to say that Augustine destroys civil authority, that it would be fairer to say that he is like Luther. For Luther said, on the one hand, that civil government is due to the Fall, but (that being granted) it is a divine ordinance; and on the other, that earthly peace and security are of such high value that no amount of civil tyranny can justify insurrection. I doubt whether S. Augustine could have agreed with Origen that 'associations of men against unjust laws are to be approved, just as we all approve associations of men to execute a tyrant who sets himself against the liberties of a State.' He must have agreed with the first proposition in so far as it refers to Christians in a pagan State.[15] But I question if he could have supported the second. So far indeed is Augustine from saying that injustice destroys the being of a commonwealth, that he uses the admitted injustice and corruption of Rome in the later days of the Republic as a *reductio ad absurdum* of Scipio's definition.

Observe, once more, that Augustine declared that his definition of a State was more probable than that of Scipio. His sense of reality led him to prefer a definition which would include all existing and historical communities, and hamper him as little as possible by an abstract ideal.

What is morally right for a nation to do is one thing. It is another thing to say, that if it fails to do it, then it ceases to be a nation. You can be human without being humane. The whole discussion is akin to that way of speaking which judges humanity, not by what it is, but by what it should be, in the developed notion of *humanitas.* It is not wise to say, even of our worst enemies, that they are not human—only that they act in a way that is a disgrace to the human race. The worst of men is a 'man for a' that.'

Augustine's second definition goes back beyond Plato. It is

paralleled by our modern distinction between law and (moral) right. What is not just is not law, said Algernon Sidney. This saying goes back through Bellarmine to S. Thomas, and through S. Thomas to S. Augustine—and further to Ulpian and the Stoics— with the definition *jus est ars aequi et boni.* We do not now talk like Algernon Sidney. We prefer to say that laws may often be unjust, but that they are still laws We have been led to develop another plan, which is true to the facts of organised government, and therefore distinguishes law sharply from moral right. All of us are familiar with the notion that law is a universal command of the governing element in a community, although it may be oppressive, immoral and irreligious. Augustine did not go so far as this, but he realised the distinction which exists between a State permeated by justice, and a despotism or democracy which is still a State, though far removed from justice. He saw that State, reduced to its lowest terms, might be a people whose 'manners are none and their customs beastly'— associated for bad ends, yet still a State, because keeping internal peace. Our distinction between legal and moral right can be derived out of this definition which allows to the community the full rights of a commonwealth, irrespective of its moral character.

On what grounds the importance of this passage is denied I fail to understand. It was well enough for mediæval writers to take the other side only and argue from it. Professedly they were trying to conduct the State as a society of baptised persons. It is less comprehensible how writers in our modern world should try to tie S. Augustine down by his own severe interpretation of Scipio's definition, an interpretation which he develops only in order to pass to a different definition. So far is S. Augustine from giving a clericalist definition of the State, that he definitely discards it, and shows us that he does so with intention, and gives his grounds. It is contrary to the facts of life.[16]

Observe that we are discussing, not what S. Augustine ought to have meant, on a view of a certain section of his words, nor what those living in a different age might get out of his language, nor even what historically was the outcome of it, but simply what was the picture of the State that Augustine had in

60

his own mind. The question is not what he has come to mean for others, but what he did mean himself.

We must do what we have to do in regard to any thinker, viz. get behind his words and stated theories, and see what were the half-conscious presuppositions of his thought. Did Augustine represent to himself that civil society is a bad thing? Is it not truer to say that he regarded it as natural—although often perverted by evil wills? He is always arguing that every nature, even that of the devil, is good as nature, but that the will to use it aright has been changed by experience. The two societies, the terrene and the divine, are made by the two loves, the love of God and the love of self apart from God. With all actual States, the latter had much to do. Romulus, like Cain, killed his brother. Historically, wrongdoing has much to say in politics. Does anyone reading the newspapers deny this? In practice a State may have often been ruled by the 'law of the beasts' described by Machiavelli—but only partly is this so, or else the idea of justice could never have arisen. Nowhere, however, does he assert that human society is a bad thing. One of his most eloquent passages describes its value. Things being what they are, wars even may be just. Augustine is no pacifist. Wars are the result of the will to power, and are evil. Yet in the actual world they may be the less of two evils. Our Lord condemns not the act of defence but the animus of revenge. The earlier wars of Rome were, acts of defence as against criminal attacks. Her Empire was a reward of relative virtue. All governments are the will of God. Christianity, he claims, will mitigate even war. He looks to the development of moral limitation on war, under definitely Christian ideals. He quotes Cicero, and dilates (in the 'Confessions,' iii. 8) upon the *generale pactum humanae societatis obedire regibus,* and is frequent in his references to the duty of obedience to civil governors as laid down by S. Paul and S. Peter. Nor does he interpret this in the hierarchical sense—a thing which was frequently done in the Middle Ages.

How then is he to be treated as hostile to the State? Felix Dahn wrote that the doctrine of S. Augustine was logically false, morally diseased, politically corrupt and incompatible with duties to the State.[17] Yet Augustine in his tractate *De Moribus*

61

Ecclesiae Catholicae, I. xxx., has a fine passage on the effects of the love of God and our neighbour in teaching every kind of civic duty:

'Tu pueriliter pueros, fortiter juvenes, quiete senes, prout cujusque non corporis tantum, sed et animi aetas est, exerces ac doces. . . .

'Tu cives civibus, gentes gentibus, et prorsus homines primorum parentum recordatione, non societate tantum, sed quadam etiam fraternitate conjungis. Doces reges prospicere populis, mones populos se subdere regibus.'

He did not, as I said earlier, set out to produce a theory of the State. There is no discussion about the merits of the various forms of government, though there is the classical passage known as the 'Mirror of Princes' describing the attributes of a good king. The one purely political passage is that which I discussed earlier in the argument for a family of small States, living in amity, with its corollary the condemnation of imperialism.

His strongest word is that passage (II. 21) in which he says, that, in the strictest view of justice, you could have only one real kingdom, that in which Christ is King. That, however, is little more than the sentiment of almost any Christian; that the best commonwealth would be composed of the people who accepted the best principles. It can hardly be said even to involve a hierarchical control. At any rate he says it, not in order to deny the rights of a commonwealth to other bodies— but to assert the need of a different classification. Still this passage would undoubtedly stimulate (as it did) the hierarchical interpretation of his doctrine. But it really illustrates the thesis of Mausbach and Seidel,[18] that Augustine did not deny the goods of human life, but sought to raise them to a higher power. That may be taken as one side. That there is another, the purely other-worldly, which treats as null all earthly activities including the State, is not to be denied on any fair reading.[19] The world-renouncing and the world-accepting temper both meet in S. Augustine, as they do in the Christian Church and its most eminent representatives, S.

Paul, S. Anselm, S. Francis de Sales, Fénelon, Newman. It must be this latter element which gives Renter the ground to state that for Augustine the only true State is a monastic community, and that all the rest are condemned ; though I do not know what real evidence there is of this statement. The former is that which can justify Mausbach[20] in saying that nothing that we call 'kultur' is recognised by S. Augustine. All this, however, can only be fully discussed if we consider the place in his system of the Christian Church. That must be taken next time.

Notes to Lecture III

[1] Seidel, *Die Lehre des heiligen Augustinus vom Staate* (in Sdralek's *Kirchengeschichtliche Abhandlungen,* 1909,IX. i.), p.4534, d.11, Band 8-10.

'Es ist wohl zu optimistisch, wenn Mausbach meint, es sei allgemein anerkannt, dass der Ausdruck *civitas terrena* meist nicht den Staat als solchen bezeichne. Meines Erachtens rühren viele Irrtümer eben gerade daher, dass man immer wieder *civitas terrena* mit "Staat" übersetzt.'

[2] Reuter, p. 131.

'Indessen scheint es mir doch nicht überflüssig zu sein, daran zu erinnern, dass das Wort nicht mit Staat, sondern *Stadt* zu übersetzen sei.'

[3] T. Sommerlad, *Das Wirtschaftsprogramm der Kirche des Mittel alters,* p. 216. (This book emphasises his differences from all forerunners. They are reactionary, he is communistic.)

'Es liegt in all dem Gesagten begründet, weshalb Augustin, der eine Staats- und Gesellschaftstheorie geben wollte, entgegen seiner Absicht ein Staatsprogramm und ein Wirtschaftsprogramm geschaffen hat.'

[4] Reuter, p. 477.

'In dem *Liber de opere monachorum,* S. 438-443, vielleicht dei bedeutendsten Schrift in der Geschichte der Wirtschaftslehre seit Ende des vierten Jahrhunderts, sind Gedanken entwickelt, welche praktisch geworden, die auch von Aug. festgehaltene Differenz des weltlichen und geistlichen Lebens hätten auflösen, eine soziale Reform (Revolution?) in römische Reiche hatten motivieren müssen.'

[5] Somerlad, *Wirtschaftsprogramm,* p. 210.

'Die Eigentümlichkeit der Staatstheorie Augustins besteht nun darin dass jene teleologische Betrachtung, wie sie das Evangelium den wirschaftlichen Institututionen gegenüber eingeschlagen hatte, auch auf die Institution des Staates angewandt wird.'

[6] Ritschl, *Ueber die Methode der älteren Dogmengeschichte,* in *Gesammette Aufsätze,* i. 156.

'Er in ihrer katholischen Gestalt das Reich Gottes selbst erkennt, welches seit dem Sündenfalle seine Existenz gegenüber dem irdischen Reiche hat; dieses aber ist der Weltstaat, wie er in der römischen Herrschaft jener Zeit gegenwärtig war. Wie nun die Kirche als die *Civitas Dei* der Organismus des Guten aus dem Prinzip der gottgemässen Gerechtigkeit ist, so gilt dem Augustin der Staat als die Gemeinschaft der Menschen aus dem Princip der Sünde.'

[7] H. von Eicken, *Geschichte und System der Mittelalterlichen Weltanschauung,* p. 119. 'So bald die Kirche sich gesetzlich geschützt sah, gab sie ihrer Geringachtung gegen den Staat einen noch offeneren, rückhaltsloseren, Ausdruck als vordem.'

[8] Reuter, p. 151.

'Man kann die Staatslehre Augustin's nur mit äusserster Vorsicht und selbst dann nicht vollständig aus den *Lib. de Civ.* schöpfen. Sie ist korrekt nur unter Vergleichung anderer Schriften, namentlich der anti-donatistischen aufzubauen.'

[9] Reuter, p. 143.

'Je schroffer die letzteren [Donatisten] die alte Ansicht von dem Staate als einem profanen, dem Christentum fremden Gemeinwesen erneuerten und überspannten, um so mehr wurde der Apologet des Katholicismus genötigt, die sittliche Würde desselben darzulegen.'

[10] *De Civitate,* xix. 23.

'Quapropter ubi non est ista justitia, ut secundum suam gratiam civitati oboedienti Deus imperet unus et summus, ne cuiquam sacrificet nisi tantum sibi; et per hoc in omnibus hominibus ad eandem civitatem pertinentibus atque oboedientibus Deo animus etiam corpori, atque ratio vitiis, ordine legitimo fideliter imperet; ut quemadmodum Justus unus, ita coetus populusque justorum vivat, ex fide quae operatur per dilectionem, qua homo diligit Deum, sicut diligendus est Deus, et proximum sicut seipsum—ubi ergo non est ista justitia, profecto non est coetus hominum juris consensu, et utilitatis communione sociatus. Quod si non est, utique populus non est, si vera est haec populi definitio. Ergo nec respublica est, quia res populi non est, ubi ipse populus non est.'

[11] Seidel, p. 21.

'Wenn also der Staat auch nicht die *veritas iustitiae* haben muss, um Staat zu sein, so muss er doch eine *iustitia* haben, um nicht als Räuberbande zu gelten. Es ist die auf der Vernunft beruhende natür-liche Gerechtigkeit, welche Augustin dem Staate als wesentlich zuschreibt. Er findet diese *iustitia* auchbei den heidnischen Römern.' *Cf.* Reuter, 137 *sqq.*

[12] Seidel, p. 20.

'Mit allem Nachdruck ist hervorzuheben, dass der heilige Augustinus die Wesensbestimmung, welche Cicero vom Staate gibt, als zu eng ablehnt.'

[13] Eckstädt, *Augustins Anschauung vom Staat* (Kirkhain, 1912), pp. 27-29, argues that the real importance lies in the word concord.

'Berücksichtigt man alle diese Stellen, so kann nach meiner Meinung gar nicht bezweifelt werden dass die concordia dem Augustin unerlässlich ist für das Wesen des Staates; und dies bestätigt sich uns

weiter, wenn wir auf das höchste Gut sehen, das Augustin für den Staat fordert: pax.'

* I do not say more than plausible, because the body which has power to change the constitution would be the Austinian sovereign. But there are two ways in the U.S.A. of altering the constitution. Which makes the sovereign?

[14] Mausbach, ii. 364.

'Also handelt es sich nicht um Umwandlung eines Bösen zum Guten, sondern um die Vermehrung und Erhöhung eines Guten.'

[15] Seidel, p. 25.

'Die Begrifie des "christlichen" oder "nichtchristlichen" Staates finden sich also nicht bei Augustin, sondern diese Bezeichnungen sind von *uns* gewählt, um vom Christentum beeinflusste oder nichtbeein-flusste Staaten zu unterscheiden.'

[16] Eckstädt, p. 40.

'So nach Augustins eigenen Urteil, ist der Staat um so besser, je besser das ist was er liebt. So ist der christliche Staat nicht dem Wesen nach der ideale Staat, wohl aber seinem Inhalte nach der Werthvollste.'

[17] F. Dahn, *Die Könige der Germanen* (Leipzig, 1908), xi. 209.

'Die Unterschätzung von Recht und Staat gegenüber der Kirche . . . ist die notwendige Folge der Lehre Sankt Augustins, einer

logisch falschen, sittlich krankhaften, politisch verderblichen,
mit den Pflichten gegen den Staat unvereinbaren.'

[18] Seidel, p. 26.

'So wird auch der Staat als naturgemässe und darum
berechtigte menschliche Ordnung durch das Übernatürliche
des Christentums nicht als unberechtigt aufgehoben, sondern
von Mängeln befreit, in seinem Wesen vervollkommnet und in
seiner Bedeutung erhöht.'

[19] H. Weinand, *Die Gottesidee der Grundzug der
Weltanschauung des hi. Augustinus,* p. 127.

'Die Welt zu entwerten stellte er sie mit all ihren Güten neben
Gott, verglich beide miteinander, wog sie gegeneinander ab ;
kein Wunder dass sie zu leicht befunden ward und ihm Gott
gegenüber als nicht-gut, nicht-schön; ja als ein Nicht-Sein
erschien.'

[20] Mausbach, i. 350.

'Was aber Augustins Stellung zur Kultur in ganzen angeht, so
unterliegt es nach unsern Untersuchungen keinem Zweifel,
dass er alle Werte und Ziele, die wir heute zum Begriffe der
Kultur rechnen, zur Geltung und zu Ehren kommen lässt.'

THE CHURCH

WHAT then is S. Augustine's view of the place of the Church in relation to civil society? This is part of the topic of the last lecture. Only to-day we look at the matter from a different angle. Here too, a *caveat* must be entered. We must beware of treating anything said of the *Civitas Dei* as though it could be applied to the existing ecclesiastical system. Much of it can. Yet the *Civitas Dei* in its strict sense is not the Visible Church. It is the *communio sanctorum,* the body of the elect, many of whom are to be found in pre-Christian times or in heathen peoples— while from this body many among the baptised will be excluded.[1] This *communio sanctorum* is the true recipient of the promises to David and of the gifts of eternal peace and beatitude, those promises which Augustine sets forth with moving eloquence in Book XX. The Visible Militant Church is never more than a part of either—nor does it ever attain. Its peace and beatitude are in hope. It is always *in via.* It is but the symbolic and inadequate representative of the *Civitas Dei,*but it uses the peace provided by the earthly State.[2] Still we must beware of laying too much stress on this. Reuter overstrains it. Augustine, it appears to be proved, is the first of the fathers to declare that the Church is the Kingdom of God on earth. The most important of the passages is that in XX. 9. There Augustine is arguing for the identification of the Church with the millennial kingdom (as against the Chiliasts) and for the rulers of the Church sitting on thrones. He says explicitly:

'Ergo ecclesia et nunc est regnum Christi regnumque caelorum.' [3]

Other passages also state this identification of the Church with the *Civitas Dei.* Reuter will have it that all these are to be

68

understood of the Church only as *communio sanctorum*.[4]
Therefore we must rule out every inference that might be drawn
from the application of the idea of the Kingdom to the actual
Church Militant. This interpretation cannot be proved. There is
little doubt, from the context, that Augustine was thinking, as
Scholz and Seidel say, of the Church as a visible,
comprehensible body, hierarchically organised.

Dr. Cunningham's Hulsean Lectures afford us an instance of
the opposite view.

'For S. Austin the Kingdom of God was not a mere hope, but a
present reality; not a mere name for a divine idea, but an
institution, duly organised among men, subsisting from one
generation to another; closely inter-connected with earthly rule,
with definite guidance to give, and a definite part to take, in all
the affairs of actual life. To him the Kingdom of God was an
actual Polity, just as the Roman Empire was a Polity too; it was
"visible" in just the same way in the earthly State, for it was a
real institution with a definite organisation, with a recognised
constitution, with a code of laws and means of enforcing them,
with property for its uses and officers to direct it.'

Here then are the two opposing views. I take another Point.
Both Reuter and Troeltsch argue that while Augustine accepted
the authority of the Church and had no wish to change it—they
were the presuppositions of his life as a Christian—yet he
meant little by them:

that his emphasis upon predestination makes against any high
view of ecclesiastical order. Repeatedly in his writings, *e.g.* in
the 'De Catechizandis Rudibus,' Augustine lays stress on the
fact that the elect will include men of all nations and every age.
At the beginning of the 'De Civitate' he declares that the *Civitas
Dei* began with the beginning of the world. Reuter (who is a
Protestant) goes so far as to say, that of all early Catholic
writers hardly any is so little hierarchically minded as
Augustine. It is true that Augustine takes little interest in
hierarchical topics. Never, so far as I know, does he develop the
theory of the episcopate in the way in which S. Cyprian did.
When he thinks of the Church, it is of the whole body of the

faithful. It is the bigness of it that appeals to him, and to which he appeals. Whatever his views in favour of small States, in regard to the Church he is imperialist enough; he is opposed to all particularism. It is to this sense of universality, rather than to that of the episcopate, that he appeals. Still, it is of the Church as an organised body, hierarchically governed, that he thinks in his controversy with the Donatists. His strong views of the predestination of individuals no more upset his scheme of a visible Church than did those of Calvin. Calvin threw over the ancient system, and rejected both the Papacy and the Episcopacy; but no less strongly than S. Augustine did he hold to a doctrine of a Visible Church and its authority. So did the Jansenists. It seems little short of ridiculous to deny that the notion of the Church loomed large to Augustine's imagination, much larger than it did to that of Origen and the earlier apologists; or that, along with the doctrine of original sin, it was the pivot of his system.[5] It had been to the Catholic Church that he had been converted after trying many experiments.

Rightly has it been pointed out by Schmidt[6] and Weinand[7] that it was the Donatist schism that aroused the Church as a society to full self-consciousness. All the earlier heresies concerned high doctrine. Certain statements about our Lord or the Trinity were, or were alleged to be, false. In opposition to them, the Church is primarily a teacher. But the Donatists were not heretics in the ordinary sense. Or rather their heresy was on the topic of the Church. Augustine was faced with (a) a doctrine of the sacraments which reduced religion to personal influence and is, in our modern phrase, radically Protestant; and (b) with the claim of the Donatist schism to be the true Church of Africa. Against these claims he was forced to develop the idea of the Church as being something more than a company of believers, as the sphere of God's work, the *Civitas Dei*; and of the sacraments as God's work done by human agents, the character of whom no more affected their validity than does that of an officer in the army the validity of his orders. Further, the Church as a universal world-wide polity is opposed to all particularist, nationalist tendencies. In the early years of the fifth century it looked as though Donatism was to be the national religion of Africa. This contest was a conflict

70

between Catholicity in its very idea, and conceptions which were its antithesis.

These ideas of S. Augustine need not have been new. It is not their novelty which makes the difference, but the emphasis with which they are stressed. Further, the term *Civitas Dei* is itself significant. This is not new. It can be seen in the New Testament, in Hebrews, and the Apocalypse. The vogue given to these words now caused more and more assimilation of the Church to a State. All the qualifications were left out of account. This process led to a political habit of treating the Church. By the mere use of the terms *civitas* and *regnum* in a work of such momentous influence, Augustine prepared the way for the later development of the doctrine that the Church is a *societas perfecta,* and must have the powers necessary to any self-sufficing community. The conception of the Church as a social entity wielding governing powers owes much to S. Augustine. He did much to strengthen the Church as an imperial force.

If we take two nineteenth-century writers, one in the East and one in the West, who thought much about the Church, Khomiakoff and Newman, what a wide gulf there is between them! Newman's sermons, in the volume of the famous fifteen on the Church as an imperial power, show how far the West has gone in this political way of thinking about the Church. Augustine may be said to have been one of the great forces which began this development. Meanwhile the East remained as it had been, preserving the view that the laity form a real part of the organisation.

Ritschl thought that Augustine's emphasis on the Church was the necessary corollary of the doctrine of original sin—the setting up of the society of grace. I cannot see this. Grace might be conceived as acting merely on the individual; and all importance be denied to the Church. Some even have based such a doctrine on S. Augustine.

But he did think that the Church, the Visible Church, recruited by baptism, nourished by sacraments, governed by bishops, was the one true family of God ; and that Christianity meant belonging to that family. The actual expression *extra ecclesiam nulla salus* is not his. But the principle he definitely states. When you add to this the view that the Church was the *regnum Dei,* and that the millennial kingdom of Christ was exercised by the rulers of the Church, you can see how much was latent in S. Augustine of the political aspect of Christianity.

More momentous is Augustine's treatment of the Church as the apocalyptic kingdom. This doctrine he develops against the Chiliasts, scouting their notion of an earthly physical reign of our Lord visible on earth. The opposing party was important at that time, and some alternative interpretation of the biblical passages was needed. Augustine seems to have taken the doctrine from Tyconius. This Tyconius was a Donatist with whom Augustine stood on friendly terms. Moreover, he had quarrelled with those of the more extreme tendencies. Augustine indeed wonders why he did not become a Catholic. In the 'Rules of Tyconius' we have found (as I said earlier) Augustine's doctrine of the two Cities, and the conception of the bipartite character of the City of God, *i.e.* consisting of the elect and the foredoomed. Above all, Augustine's interpretation of the Apocalypse is found to be derived from Tyconius, who wrote a treatise on the Apocalypse, which now has been lost, but has been partly restored by conjecture.

The point of this exposition is that the millennial kingdom is already in existence. It is a reign, therefore, that does not involve the physical presence of Christ. In other words, the Second Coming is the Church. The First Resurrection has already taken place in the conversion of sinners and in their baptism. It is a spiritual act, not a physical resurrection. In his interpretation of Scripture Augustine oscillates between extreme literalism and a remarkable freedom. The martyrs are those who reign with Christ. The thrones belong to the rulers of the Church. This kingdom has been in existence ever since Christianity spread beyond Judaea. It has nothing to do with the peace of the Church and the cessation of persecution, still less with the legal establishment of Christianity. Neither persecution nor any other earthly act affects this.

The ground for rejecting Chiliasm is that it postulates an

72

absence of earthly trials in this life—a thing which Augustine declares to be no less impossible for saints than anyone else: and for that reason the promises that there shall be no more sorrow nor crying can apply only to the Church Triumphant. Now this argument cuts two ways. If the Church be the Kingdom of God, it may, it is held, justify claims to paramount supremacy, and lead to a great Church-State. A more natural interpretation points the other way. If Christ has been reigning on earth, through the Church, ever since the days of Antioch, then he was reigning all through the period of persecution. Therefore for the Church to exercise any political supremacy, or even secure any recognition of its existence, are shown to be things indifferent. The royalty of the Church, 'the peculiar people, the holy nation, the royal priesthood,' the power on earth of the King of Kings and Lord of Lords, is of the same nature as that of which Christ spoke when He answered Pilate's satirical question—'Art thou a King then 'with' My Kingdom is not of this world.' The Kingdom of God cometh not by observation, and its authority is in the souls of men, not in any outward political structure. It was regal in her days of security, regal when she was a distinct society in the second century, regal when she was assailed by the whole might of Rome under Diocletian, regal when having conquered by stooping she enjoyed a guaranteed security, regal when under Julian that security was threatened once more, or when under Arians, like Constantius or Valens, it was undermined from within, regal no more and no less than it had been previously now that after the laws of Gratian and Theodosius she had become not merely tolerated but established, not merely established but the exclusive official religion of the Empire.

The Church is a kingdom not of this world. Augustine goes out of his way to say that kings and princes cannot make the City of God, which comes by the calling of souls. Once more it must be said that Augustine was not thinking how to build Jerusalem in Afric's bright and sunny land, but how to wean men from 'crying "peace, peace" when there was no peace,' from seeking in any earthly refuge that abiding home which remaineth for the people of God. Richard Baxter's great book, 'The Saints' Everlasting Rest,' reflects the aim and many of the ideas of S. Augustine or the famous poem of Bernard of Murles, from which is taken the hymn 'Jerusalem the Golden.' This non-political interpretation of the symbolic kingdom is seen to be that which is in accordance with the mind of S. Augustine, if we take the book as a whole. It is what he meant to mean; whether it is always what his words did mean, is another question.

But evidence that tells on the other side is not to be neglected. First, it is obviously possible to put a clericalist interpretation upon the passages about justice. Next, it must be remembered that he speaks of the good that has been done to the Church by Christian kings. In reply to Petilian he says that he does not give unreserved trust to the State, but makes use of it. He admits the change which had come over the Empire since Constantine. He says that, since ruling is the *métier* of princes, they, if they come over to the Church, must forward her interests by laws in her favour. In other places he speaks of the duty of the civil governor to do what the Church requires in her interests. Now one commentator thinks that all this amounts to not much less than the comparison of Church and State to sun and moon, which was first found, I think, in Hildebrand,[8] and became so dear to the Middle Ages. But I confess that I can see nothing here that in any sense approaches to the doctrine of the two swords, or even to the famous argument of Gelasius.

The Church was not yet in a condition even of parity with the civil power. Augustine does not think of the civil and ecclesiastical authorities as two co-ordinate Powers occupied in governing. Even in dream he had not the great vision of mediæval imagination, the one commonwealth of Catholic Christians, with its twin heads of Pope and Emperor; though he does say that there is one *respublica* of all Christians. It is doubtful whether he hoped to convert the heathen by force, though he asks the Donatists whether they did not agree with him in approving the imperial laws against heathen sacrifice. Augustine appeals to the unity of the Church, the *Civitas Dei* alike in morals and thought and sets this against the intellectual and moral anarchy of the terrene State; yet he is not at that moment thinking of an imperial Christ-state, but pointing to actual phenomena as a modern Roman Catholic in England or the United States might do. Yet it is not doubtful that it was possible in later times, and indeed natural, to press all this into the service of the hierarchical organisation of the world.

Most of Augustine's writing is not in the tone of a ruling Church, but rather of a body officially predominant, though everywhere attacked. His attitude to Count Boniface is not like that of the mediæval popes.

It is the other world with which he is concerned. He might have called his book 'The Gospel of the Resurrection.' The 'De Civitate Dei' is chargeable with whatever plaints can be made against a tendency to other-world lines. The strongest passage on this point is not to be found there, but in the 'De Bono Conjugali.' Answering the objection that if his views were correct, and if enough people became converted to the celibate life, the world could not go on being peopled, for no children would be born, he replies: 'That would be a blessing. It would mean that the number of the elect would be filled up, and the kingdom of God accomplished'—in the language of our Burial Service. This presumably alludes to the theory that the world need only go on until the number of elect required to fill up the vacancies caused by the falling of the angels had been made up. That was the object of the creation—to fill up the gaps in heaven. The rest do not matter. God would not keep the factory of the world running for the sake of the waste-products. You may fairly urge against S. Augustine the kind of reproaches that figure in the Pagan's Lament in Swinburne's poem:

> 'Thou hast conquered, O pale Galilean, and the world has
>   grown grey with Thy breath;
> We have drunken of things Lethean, and fed on the kisses
>   of death.'

But it is a different charge to make him 'the only begetter' of the Bull, *Unam sanctam.*

That is not to deny that there are weighty considerations in favour of such a view. Were there not, we could never have such strong words as those of Kattenbusch, who speaks of him as the Father of the Papacy. Geirke holds that the logical development of the Augustinian doctrine involves the complete subjection of the State to the Church.[9] Similar are the views of Dorner, Schmidt, Eicken and many more.[10] Their views are stronger evidence of what Augustine meant, than is the constant use that was made of him by mediæval thinkers. The mediæval habit of taking tags as text-proofs, apart from the general purpose of the writer, discounts their value as evidence. Besides this there was an immediate polemical interest at stake.

For this purpose we must go further. The 'De Civitate Dei' needs for its interpretation the writings against the Donatists. In that conflict Augustine was led to accept the assistance of the civil power. So far as I can make out, he was never very happy about this proceeding, and felt that it needed apology. Partly, this feeling was due to the fact that his action indicated a definite change of mind. In early days, and in regard to the controversy with the Manichæans, Augustine had forgone all such things, and argued in favour of freedom of opinion. This was a change, and one which he had to explain. So far as the Donatists were concerned, he had an easy task. From them indeed any objection to the employment of force was little short of an impertinence. They had themselves appealed to the civil power. Only when the appeal was rejected had they turned round and cried 'hands off' to the State. Besides the violence of the Circumcellions, if not precisely authorised, was largely used by them. Much of what was done on the side of the Church was only an attempt often ineffectual, to secure that the peace should be kept. This attempt had been largely frustrated through the intimacy between Optatus and the Count Gildo.

Augustine did not confine his defence to these limits. He produced a definite argument in favour of force in religious matters. Most of it he bases on the verse 'Compel them to come in.' He does not want opinion forced. He thinks that penalty is useful, because it makes a man reflect, and often give up his view as erroneous. It is, in fact, educational, and, in his view, precisely similar to the use of the rod. It is persecution for the soul's good. Augustine's conception of the office of the State is largely that of an educator.

76

Out of this acceptance of persecution it is easy to develop a theory of civil domination. The State is to use force. That is its duty. It is to extend the province of the Kingdom of God on earth. Remember, it is not, as it was later on, conceived as being the 'secular arm' of the Church. If the civil Governor is to persecute heresy, who is to advise him? He cannot do so on his own motion. Obviously, the Church, organised through its governors, will advise him. The moment you accept persecution as a policy, you tend to a religious tyranny. The State may still be conceived as having self-identity of its own—as it was in the Presbyterian doctrine of the two kingdoms. But if it be bound to take orders from the Church in regard to religious matters, it will not be long before there will be a claim to direct the State in regard to any policy that may have a religious, or a moral, or an ecclesiastical bearing. How much will be left out?

Add to this the inferences that may be drawn from justice (as Augustine defines it) as being needful to a perfect commonwealth. If the only true commonwealth be that in which Christ is King, and if that is to mean that the worship of God in Christ is not merely to be allowed, but to be enjoined by law, then you must have a theocratic State. It depends merely on what form of organisation the Church has, as to who shall have the last word. In a democratic system you might have the whole body of the faithful. In a hierarchical Church you might have either a General Assembly as in Scotland, or a General Council of bishops—or the Pope. As we saw last time, that notion of justice is not at all S. Augustine's own doctrine of the State. But it was sufficiently near it for men to take it apart from the rest; and, together with other indications, to make it serve the ends of the clericalism of the later Middle Ages.

Even more is this true with regard to the conception of the Church as the apocalyptic kingdom. If the Church be, here and now, in enjoyment of its millennial glory, then the largest terms of supremacy that can be brought out of the Apocalypse may be interpreted literally. Its earthly head will be King of Kings and Lord of Lords.

All these elements together—(a) the doctrine of a religion using the force of a *compelle intrare,* which must give to the Church some claim to dictate what shall be persecuted as heresy; (*b*) the doctrine of justice as necessary to a State, together with S. Augustine's glosses, leading to a control of all law for spiritual ends; (*c*) the doctrine of the Church as a polity, as the millennial Kingdom of Christ, implying a reigning authority—will tend to develop a state of mind which will picture the *Civitas Dei* as a christianised Church-State, from which unbelievers are excluded, and which would claim, directly or indirectly, the supreme power in that State for the leaders of the hierarchy. If we add to this the effects of the Church's long continuance in a concentration upon earthly activities, the development of vast administrative machinery, the fact that she became to the conquering barbarians the symbol and the source of all culture, we are well on our way to such a conception of church-power as was represented by Innocent III.

Notes to Lecture IV

[1] Reuter, p. 151.

'Die *Libri de Civitate Dei* haben nicht den direkten Zweck, die Frage nach "dem Verhältnis der christlichen Kirche zum Staate," im Sinne des heutigen Sprachgebrauchs zu beantworten, sondern sind prinzipiell zum Zwecke der Verteidigung der Christentums (der christlichen Kirche) gegen das Heidentum abgefasst.

'Die *Civitas terrena* bedeutet erstens den heidnischen Staat, zweitens, die bis zum Ende der Welt, also auch in der christlichen Zeit bestehende *societas improborum*.

'Die *Civitas Dei* ist erstens die historische sichtbare Kirche—zweitens die *communio sanctorum (electorum)*.'

[2] *De Civitate,* xix. 17.

'Haec ergo coelestis civitas dum peregrinatur in terra, ex

omnibus gentibus cives evocat, adque in omnibus linguis peregrinam colligit societatem, non curans quidquid in moribus legibus institutisque diversum est, quibus pax terrena vel conquiritur vel tenetur, nihil eorum rescindens vel destruens, immo etiam servans ac sequens; quod licet diversum sit in diversis nationibus, ad unum tamen eundemque finem terrenae pacis intenditur, si religionem qua unus summus et verus Deus colendus docetur, non impedit.

'Utitur ergo etiam coelestis civitas, in hac sua peregrinatione, pace terrena, et de rebus ad mortalem hominum naturam pertinentibus, humanarum voluntatum compositionem, quantum salva pietate ac religione conceditur, tuetur adque adpetit, eamque terrenam pacem refert ad coelestem pacem; quae vere ita pax est, ut rationalis dumtaxat creaturae sola pax habenda adque dicenda sit, ordinatissima scilicet et concordissima societas fruendi Deo et invicem in Deo; quo cum ventum fuerit, non erit vita mortalis, sed plane certeque vitalis; nee corpus animale quod dum corrumpitur aggravat animam, sed spiritale sine ulla indigentia ex omni parte subditum voluntati. Hanc pacem, dum peregrinatur in fide, habet, adque ex hac fide juste vivit, cum ad illam pacem adipiscendam refert quidquid bonarum actionum gerit erga Deum et proximum, quoniam vita civitatis utique socialis est.'

[3] F. Kattenbusch, *Kritische Studien zur Symbolik*, p. 200.

'In dem Augustinischen Kirchenbegriff wird gewöhnlich ein Gedanke übersehen, der aber doch von der höchsten Tragweite ist. Das ist der dass die Kirche das tausendjährige Reich und in so fern bereits das Reich Gottes darstellt.'

[4] Reuter, p. 150.

'Die Formel, "die Kirche ist das Reich Gottes" ist prinzipiell nicht von der verfassungsmässig organisierten, von den Bischöfen regierten Kirche ausgesagt, sondern von derjenigen, welche als *communio sanctorum* vorgestellt wird, bestimmter von dem Teile derselben —denn der Grundbestandtheil gehört dem Himmel an—welcher hier auf Erden sich befindet.'

Cf. also Schmidt (*Jahrbücher,* vi. 238)—Die Kirche ist in erster Linie Leib Christi als *Communio Sanctorum.*

Scholz, *Glaube und Unglaube,* 119. Criticises Reuter's view of *regnum Dei* as equivalent to *communio sanctorum,* and points to Augustine's use of Tyconius.

[5] Reuter, p. 499.

'Durch Augustin ist die Idee der Kirche in einer Weise, die dem Orient fremd geblieben, die Zentralmacht in der religiösen Stimmung, in dem kirchlichen Handeln des Abendlandes geworden. Sein eigenes Denken war allerding beherrscht worden dutch jene andere, welche wir oben (S. 97) nachgewiesen haben; aber die Formel "die Kirche ist das Reich Gottes," schon von ihm nicht immer in dem genuinen Sinne gebraucht, früh von anderen in Widerspruch mit der ursprünglichen Intention des Verfassers verstanden, ist thatsächlich wider seine Absicht das Fundament der Ansprüche der römischen Hierarchic, "das Programm jener römisch-katholischen Weltherrschaft," an welche Augustin nie gedacht hatte—die Schwungkraft des Gregorianismus geworden.'

[6] Schmidt, H., *Des Augustinus Lehre von der Kirche,* in *Jahrbücher für Deutsche Theologie,* vi. p. 198.

'Das Selbstbewusstsein der Kirche konnte sich vollständiger nur entwickeln, wenn es sich nicht allein der Härese, sondern auch dem Schisma gegenüber auszusprechen hatte.'

This situation was produced by the Donatist controversy: and this helped to mould the Church into a State-religion.

[7] Weinand, pp. 109, no.

'(Augustin hat) den Kreis der Kirche weit über den Rahmen der sichtbaren Gemeinde erweitert. Wie weitherzig das zeigt die Grundauffassung der *Civitas Dei,* die Kirche sei so alt wie die Welt. *Res ipsa quae nunc Christiana religio nuncupatur erat apud antiques, nee defuit ab initio generis humani.*'

[8] Kattenbusch, p. 197.

'In so fern ist doch Augustin der Vater auch des Papsttums,' p. 201. 'Wir haben in jenem Gedanken Augustins den eigentlichen Rechtstitel und das leitende Motiv für die Politik, welche die Päpste bis auf die Gegenwart festhalten. Diese Politik ist eben nichts anderes, als die rücksichtslose kühne, wenn man will, grossartige und imposante Durchführung der Idee, dass die Kirche als das Reich Gottes die berufene Herrin aller Verhältnisse sei.'

Ritschl, i. 166.

'Daran sind in der Lehre von der obersten Auctorität der Kirche die Ideen nachzuweisen, auf Grund deren der römische Primat sich über den Episkopat erhob und die Stellvertretung Gottes in sich zu concentriren unternahm. Ist auch Augustin kein absichtlicher Urheber dieser Entwickelung, so war sie doch durch seine Ansicht, dass die Kirche die *Civitas Dei* sei, veranlasst. Und diesen Primat an Gottes Statt haben ja die mittelaltrigen Vertreter desselben in Praxis und Theorie an einem Verhältniss zwischen Kirche und Staat durchzu-führen gesucht, dessen Bestimmung direkt von den Grundsätzen Augustin's abstammt, und, wie die Gegenwart bestätigt, dogmatischen Werth hat, also auch in der Dogmengeschichte vorgetragen werden muss.'

[9] Gierke, *Das deutsche Genossenschaftsrecht,* iii. 124.

'In der konsequenten Ausgestaltung, die sie durch Augustinus erfuhr, erkannte diese Theorie ausschliesslich den unmittelbar von Gott gestifteten und geleiteten Verband der universellen und einheitlichen Kirche, den " Staat dessen König Christus ist," als Ausdruck der sittlichen Weltordnung an. Sie liess daher den weltlichen Staat mit alien seinen Gliederungen und Einrichtungen nur gelten insofern derselbe sich dem in der Kirche realisirten göttlichen Staat, als dienender Bestandtheil ein- und unterordnete. Sie postulirte den Christlichen Staat und verstand unter dem Christlichen Staat einen Staat, welcher ausschliesslich in der Kirche die Quelle und das Ziel seiner Existenz erblickte.'

[10] Dorner, p. 303.

'Mit einem Worte, nur der der Kirche dienende Staat, welcher
die wahre Gottesverehrung schützt, entspricht seinem Begriff,
und vermag in seiner Sphäre etwas Erspriessliches zu leisten.
Dass der Staat ein eigenes in sich werthvolles Princip, eine
göttliche Idee seinerseits vertrete, erkennt Augustin nicht. Seine
Ansicht vom Staate ist nicht weit von dem Satze entfernt, dass
er der Mond sei, welcher von der Sonne seinen Glanz
empfange.'

THE 'DE CIVITATE DEI'
IN THE MIDDLE AGES

SO far we have been trying to find out what S. Augustine meant to himself. In these two closing lectures I want to consider what later ages have made of him. This is not easy. Students, and students alone, have sufficient data for a judgment concerning the practical influence of a book. Yet that often makes them bad judges. Living among books they are apt to over-estimate their significance. They may attribute to a book results which are due to many other causes. If we mean by the influence of the 'De Civitate Dei' that it caused people to think or to do things which, except for it they would not have thought or done, the problem of estimating that influence is hard to solve. As a rule no single cause is adequate, but many causes combine to produce a practical result of any historical importance. Commonly a book, however influential, is never more than a secondary cause. Rousseau did not produce the French Revolution, however highly you rate his influence. That was the consequence of forces that had been active for a long time. Rousseau may have lit the match—set fire to the powder magazine. He did not make the powder.

So with the 'De Civitate Dei.' Vast is its influence; still we must beware of the negative proposition, that if it had not been written, the course of mediæval history would have been materially different. It might have been. But it would be hard to prove this.

There is another way in which the problem is difficult—a way in which the problem about the influence of Voltaire or Rousseau is not difficult. Literally immeasurable has been the influence of S. Augustine in moulding the mind of Western Europe. So deeply has it entered into our life, that it is not possible to say where his influence begins and where it ends. For the mediæval world he summed up so much of their heritage from the ancient world—he was so large a conduit-pipe—that it is hard to say where the stream did not penetrate. His characteristic theological doctrine is so universal and of such immense import in the West, that it is easy to over-estimate it in comparison with others.

The problem of Augustine's political or semi-political influence is a little easier. It is more sharply defined. Yet even here it is hard to disentangle the threads: or to be sure that what we see at work is the mind of S. Augustine, and not other causes. Add to this the additional difficulty which is created by the mediæval habit of citing names and stock quotations merely to fortify itself, perhaps too with little acquaintance with a writer's mind.

Perhaps it is safer to say that we are examining the prevalence of certain ideals, of which S. Augustine was, or was believed to be, the exponent; and that therefore presumably had to do with their prevalence. Even Troeltsch, who is all for treating S. Augustine as above everything an ancient, admits his importance for the future—as being the founder of the first great *Kultur-Ethik* of Christendom. To-day I shall try and estimate his influence in the Middle Ages, and in the last lecture I shall deal with later times. All that can be attempted is to take certain characteristic illustrations from the earlier, the middle and the later period.

Einhard was the biographer and son-in-law of Charlemagne. I see no objection to calling him that—we need not be haunted by Freeman's ghost. In his personal description he tells us that Charlemagne was fond of reading, and more especially was devoted to the books of S. Augustine's 'De Civitate Dei.' We cannot treat this statement as being without significance. Doubtless Charles felt that the portrait of a Christian prince drawn in the Fifth Book and known as 'The Mirror of Princes,' was the portrait of the kind of prince he would like to be ('De Civitate,' V. 24):

'The State and Truth of a Christian Emperor's Felicity.— For we

Christians do not say that Christian Emperors are happy because they have a long reign, or die leaving their sons in quiet possession of their empires, or have been ever victorious, or powerful against all their opposers. These are but gifts and solaces of this laborious, joyless life; idolaters and such as belong not to God (as these Emperors do) may enjoy them; because God in His mercy will not have these that know Him to believe that such things are the best goods He gives. But happy they are (say we) if they reign justly, free from being puffed up with the glossing exaltations of their attendance or the cringes of their subjects; if they know themselves to be but men, and remember that; if they make their power their trumpeter, to divulge the true adoration of God's majesty; if they love, fear and honour Him; if they long most for that empire where they need not fear to have partners; if they be slack to avenge, quick to forgive; if they use correction for the public good, and not for private hate; if their pardons promise not liberty of offending, but indeed only hope of reformation; if they counterpoise their enforced acts of severity with the like weight of bounty and clemency; if their lusts be the lesser, because they have the larger licence; if they desire to rule their own effects, rather than others' estates; and if they do all things, not for glory, but for charity, and with all, and before all, give God the due sacrifice of prayer for their imperfections; such Christian emperors we call happy, here in hope, and hereafter when the time we look for comes, indeed.'

We may go further. Charles would not think of himself as head of a *Civitas terrena*. He need not. He aimed at a realm in which Christ was King, in which the true God was worshipped, and none other; a common-wealth inspired by justice in the strict sense, including all the theological implications of S. Augustine. That is to say, the realm of 'imperial Charlemagne' was a Christian Empire, the City of God on earth. Certainly Charles did not draw from this any doctrine of the political power of the Pope—rather he deduced the rights of imperial oversight. We may be sure that he would not classify his realm under the second definition of the commonwealth, from which justice and religion are excluded. How could he? He had baptised the Saxons at the point of the sword, and had summoned the Council of Frankfort. Proud as he may have been at being the successor of Augustus, he would regard himself yet more proudly as the successor of Constantine and Theodosius. Now Augustine (however you interpret him) never identified the *Civitas Dei* with any earthly State. But he had prepared the way for other people to do this.

The Holy Roman Empire, as it developed, declared by its first title its claim to be the *Civitas Dei* on earth— *i.e.* a true Catholic Commonwealth with two swords in all governing departments, the secular and the spiritual. Augustine could say *Omnium Christianorum una respublica est* (XXV. 1).

Charlemagne, and still more the great Otto, would feel that they were undertaking to realise that maxim in actual life. That is the meaning of the imperial claim to be 'Lord of the World.' Lord Bryce declares that 'it is hardly too much to say that the Holy Roman Empire was built upon the foundation of the "De Civitate Dei."' This statement goes too far, if by it we understand anything that S. Augustine intended. Further, it underrates the other-worldly character of S. Augustine's own conception of the *Civitas Dei*. But it is no whit short of the truth, if we adopt that interpretation of the 'De Civitate Dei,' and of the chapters upon justice as essential to a true republic, which I discussed in Lecture III. Remember too, that this—the notion of the 'great State' of the Middle Ages as the *Civitas Dei*— has nothing to do with the question whether Augustine taught a doctrine of hierarchical domination or no. It is equally compatible with Caesaro-papism. The conception of the Holy Roman Empire as of the one Commonwealth of God could claim to realise the Augustinian ideal merely by its doctrine of the ecclesiastical position of the Emperor, who is a sacred person, Canon of S. Peter's, advocate and protector of the Church. What is capital for our purpose is the point which Lord Bryce emphasises, the religious character of the Holy Roman Empire. It is not the religious character of one section (the Church so-called) set over against the other. It is the whole people, as it is the whole of life, which is gathered into one great unity. To quote in substance from one authority, Engelbert of Admont,[1] who will come again into question later on:

'"There is one and one only Commonwealth of the whole

86

Christian people. Therefore there must necessarily be one and one only king and prince of that Commonwealth, ordained and constituted for the expansion and defence of that Faith and people." On which grounds Augustine concludes that outside the Church there never was nor ever could be a true Empire, although there have been Emperors, *qualitercunque et secundum quid, non simpliciter,* who were outside the Catholic Faith and Church.'

The grandiose conception of organised human life, which was expressed in the Holy Roman Empire, was the origin of the attempts of theorists to secure a harmony. The Church and the State might serve as names for the two great departments, ecclesiastical and civil. In that way the word Church came to acquire one of its meanings—one which has never quite gone from it—as the equivalent of the clergy. But it is the Christian world as a whole, 'the whole body of Christian people throughout the world,' that is the entire Church, and makes up the entire Commonwealth. So much so that towards the close of the Middle Ages one great and revolutionary scholastic, William of Ockham, could go further even than S. Augustine's phrase about all Christians making one commonwealth, and boldly declare that all men are one society. 'Omnes homines sunt unum corpus et unum collegium.' As one writer put it, the *regnum,* the *sacerdotium,* the *studium*—the State, the Church, the University—were the rulers of the Commonwealth. This point is one which it is important to make clear before we proceed to the various controversies between the two sets of officers, civil and spiritual. Whether you take the Imperialist or the Papalist view, as to which of these is to have the last word, whether you are Erastian or clericalist, you are equally within the limits and the circle of ideas of the 'De Civitate Dei,' as it was interpreted to mean a great Church-State. Modern Erastianism is a bastard growth. It has nothing to do with the pure milk of the word dispersed by Thomas Lüber, who said that he was considering only a State in which one religion and one only was tolerated, and that the true one. But I must not linger over this. In earlier papers on 'Erastus' on the 'Respublica Christiana' I have tried to work it out in detail.[2]

Let us pass to some later illustrations. The concordant

government of the world by Pope and Emperor was an ideal. In practice there was a struggle for preponderance. The Papacy had sunk to its lowest in the tenth century. From that degradation the Saxon Emperors rescued it. The friendship between Otto the Third and Pope Sylvester II (Gerbert) did for moment realise the ideal. They write ecstatically to one another: 'Nostrum, nostrum est imperium Romanum.' Once more the Papacy drooped. The Franconian kings began to lift it from the dust. After the Synod of Sutri in 1046 and the deposition of Pope Gregory VI at the bidding of Henry III, the Cluniac revival spread through Western Europe, and its greatest representative assumed the tiara as Gregory VII. The conflict that had long been preparing now broke forth. After a brief space of amity with the weak and vicious Henry IV, Gregory launched the excommunication, and the long war began. Nowadays we are bidden not to call it the Investiture Controversy, though that is no bad name for the first phase, which ended with the Concordat of Worms in 1122. Here more than anywhere can we trace the influence of S. Augustine. Dr. Mirbt has examined all the literature.[3] In an interesting tractate he has shown how on every kind of topic S. Augustine's authority was invoked. In the 'Libelli de Lite,' which make up three volumes of the 'Monumenta Germaniae Historica,' we have an ample pamphlet literature. Augustine is used as an authority by both sides. It should be said that it is doubtful how far many of the disputants had read the 'De Civitate Dei.' Mirbt has made it clear that in this as in other matters they used collections of passages. One such collection is known. Probably there were others.[4]

The use of Augustine by both sides is evidence to justify what I said earlier, that the question of the influence of the ideal of the 'De Civitate Dei ' is irrelevant to the topic of its clericalist or regalist interpretation. Obviously Augustine can be made use of by clericalists. But when we remember that the Empire is regarded as the Commonwealth of which Christ is King, and that it is by no means certain whether Augustine could set Pope above King in any political sense, we need not be surprised that some of Hildebrand's adversaries made as much play with Augustine's name as did his supporters. One treatise among many, the 'De Unitate Ecclesiae,'[5] written after the death of

Gregory VII, we may take as an illustration. It is strongly imperialist. A passionate appeal for unity alike in Church and Empire, it is an argument in favour of the anti-pope. With arguments drawn from the maxim *remota justitia quid regna nisi magna latrocinia,* the Hildebrandine party is condemned for the deposition of Henry IV. (The writer appears to separate *ecclesia* from *regnum.* That may be because he takes *ecclesia* in the narrow sense as equivalent to the clergy.) Many and long are the citations from the 'De Civitate Dei.' The writer quotes the 'Mirror of Princes' at length, and shows that he has no doubt about the relevancy of the book to the controversy.

In Hildebrand himself we find but little use of S. Augustine. One of his earlier letters shows that he was imbued with a conception of the relations of Pope and Emperor, which could preserve the unity of the ancient ideal. The most famous letter of all points the other way. Hildebrand revives what had fallen into disuse—the non-Christian way of treating the secular State. The famous letter[6] (it is really a tract) to Hermann of Metz is akin to Augustine's account of the lust of power, as being one of the chief contributary causes to the growth of the *terrene state.* Hackneyed as is the quotation, it is needful here:

'Who,' he asks, 'is ignorant that kings and princes had their origin in those who, ignorant of God and covering themselves with pride, violence and perfidy, in fact nearly every crime, under the inspiration of the devil, the prince of this world, claimed to rule over their peers, *i.e.* men, in blind lust and intolerable arrogance.'

It is hard to suppose that Gregory was ignorant of the 'De Civitate Dei,' though the only passage from Augustine's writings which he quotes in this letter is from the 'De Doctrina Christiana.'

Another passage is even more noteworthy:

'It would really be more fitting to speak of good Christians as Kings, than to call bad princes so. The former in seeking the glory of God rule themselves. The latter seeking their own lusts are enemies to themselves and tyrants to others. The former are the body of that true King, Christ; the latter are the body of their father the devil.'

This suggests Tyconius.

Hildebrand, thinking of rulers in an ascending feudal hierarchy, could not make any special exception for royalty, and was justified by the facts of the eleventh century. Much that he said was due to his thinking of phenomena which were before his eyes. Yet in these two passages there is a very distinctive mark, as of the two cities. Also it is one of the rare mediæval passages which speak of civil government as equivalent to nothing better than the *civitas terrena*; though even here it is not civil government itself, but the actual personal wickedness of kings and princes that is condemned. Moreover, even the letter which was called out by the stress of the collision with Henry IV did not represent Gregory's whole mind. In an earlier letter he had spoken in the usual way of two coordinate and fraternal powers. In his letters to William I and other kings he seemed ready enough to adopt a high view of secular authority, provided that it is always duly subordinate to the spiritual.[7]

On the whole the controversial literature of the day witnesses to the enormous dependence on S. Augustine; and this dependence is greater in some of the other writers than it is in Hildebrand himself.

Let us pass from this to a different atmosphere, less clouded with controversy. The 'Concordia Discordantium Canorum' or 'Decretum' of Gratian (1139), although it is printed foremost in the 'Corpus Juris Canonici,' is not an authoritative work. Unlike the 'Decretale' of Gregory IX a century later, or the 'Sext' of Boniface VIII, it is not definitely promulgated law—though it must be remembered that even these decretals are in the Bulls which promulgated them, merely addressed to the University of Bologna, and not promulgated to the judges in the Courts Christian. Gratian's work is like the 'Institutes' of Coke—immense in influence but not official. It gives no legal authority to any text in it. Yet its importance is little less than if it were official. Anyhow it is evidence of the way in which the legal mind of that day looked at these matters. In this book we are in a different atmosphere. If you take the conflict between Popes and Emperors as a whole, what establishes itself is the influence of S. Augustine upon both sides, owing to the universal belief in the Empire as a Christian commonwealth, the embodiment of true justice, *i.e.* to the general repudiation of the second or minimising definition (Augustine's own) of a *respublica.* 'The mediæval Church was a State' is a common saying. Yet more true is it to say that the mediæval State was a Church—at least in ideal; for the ideal was the Holy Empire with its twin heads, the smaller semi-national states being altogether on a lower level, like duchies.

The 'Decretum' of Gratian is concerned not so much with the ideal of a Catholic Commonwealth, as with the supremacy of the ecclesiastical element over the civil. Gratian's work is more than what it seems— a compilation, more even than a law book. It is designed to make law by declaring it; it is a politico-ecclesiastical pamphlet, and mirrors the life and thought of the day. Its fundamental thesis, the subordination of civil to ecclesiastical authority, is stated at the outset. In Distinction X Gratian lays down in his own words that the constitutions of princes do not prevail over ecclesiastical constitutions; that the tribunals of kings are subject to the sacerdotal power. This statement might conceivably be explained to refer only to matters of spiritual import, and in emergency could be so explained. But Gratian meant more than that. His object was to make a law book for the Church that should be parallel with the 'Corpus Juris Civilis.' His work was executed at Bologna, the home of the great Romanist revival: it emanated from the chair which Professor Galante holds to-day. If the Pope were truly sovereign, the halting references to spiritual authority in the civil law—even those conditioned by the maxim that the Emperor was the source of all law—might have something set over against them. Justinian might begin his code with the title 'De Summa Trinitate et Fide Catholica.' That would have been enough, and more than enough, to satisfy S. Augustine. But Justinian himself had asserted an imperial supremacy in theological controversies which the Church in the West would not admit.

Here, however, we are concerned with nothing but S.

Augustine's political influence. Of the citations which make up the 'Decretum,' 530 come from his writings. Only about a dozen are out of the 'De Civitate Dei.' Many of them are of no importance. Some are of incalculable import. Comparatively little use may be made of the 'De Civitate Dei'; but this lack is more than made up by the quotations from the treatises against the Donatists. In vulgar journalese, the author has 'gutted ' the anti-Donatist treatises of S. Augustine (c. xxiii. q. iv. 37-44). The section dealing with persecution is largely made up from them. Skilful but not unfair use is made of S. Augustine's concessions. We have, it is true, no right to say that Augustine would have approved the capital punishment of heretics or of the mediæval inquisition (which was later than Gratian). But, as we saw, Augustine admitted the use of compulsion, and argued that the only reason why it was not employed by the early Christians was their numerical weakness. Another passage often thought to be an anticipation of the original contract occurs in the 'Confessions,' and is given by Augustine from Cicero, *Generale pactum humanae societatis obedire regibus.* It is S. Augustine again (in his sermon on the Centurion's son) who is cited in justification of lawful war (c. xxiii. i. 2) together with three other passages. The 'Decretum' of Gratian is one of the most important elements in the construction of mediæval society. The use it makes of Augustine's maxims in all political and semi-political matters is decisive as to his influence.

After this it may seem needless to allude to a merely literary effort. The 'Chronicon' of Otto of Freisingen, the historian of Frederic Barbarossa, was mentioned in its place in discussing S. Augustine's philosophy of history. It is an interesting illustration of the twelfth century. Otto sets himself deliberately to relate the history of the world on the line of the 'De Civitate Dei' with the help of Augustine and Orosius. The most interesting pieces are the prologues. In that prefixed to Book III there is a balanced and reflective estimate of the 'Praeparatio Evangelica,' as afforded by the universal empire of Rome. The prologue to Book IV contains a moderate statement of the imperialist position. There are two powers in the Church. Otto never puts out the idea of two distinct societies of Church and State, as was done in later times. It is with him (as always in the Middle Ages) a question of the balance of two powers in the same society. Christ desired the two swords to be in the hands of two different representatives: He uses the 'render to Cæsar' to support the rights of the crown, and quotes the pertinent passage of S. Augustine addressed to the Donatists in which he laid down that property can be rightly possessed only by human law at the bidding of kings, who are of divine appointment. Kings he holds to reign by the ordination of God and the election of the people, and Constantine with the approval of the Church *ecclesiae juste regalia contulisse.*

In the prologue to Book V he admits that the two cities have coalesced into one—the Church, with its content of tares and wheat.

'Henceforward, since not merely every nation, but the princes also with few exceptions, became Catholics, I seem to myself to have composed the history no longer of two cities, but almost entirely of one—*i.e.* which I call the Church. For I should not, as before, speak of these two cities, as two (since the elect and the reprobate are now in one home), but strictly as one, but of a mixed sort as grain together with chaff.'

In the prologue to Book VI, after lamenting the arrogance of the hierarchy who seek to strike the kingdom with that sword, which they only hold through the favour of kings, he goes on to say that he must not be taken as intending to separate the Empire from the Church, since in the Church of God the two functions, the sacerdotal and the regal, are known to exist; and he refers to his previous statement, that the history now relates to one society only. In the prologue to Book VIII he once more repeats his acknowledgment to S. Augustine, This last book is occupied with discussion of the last things, like the later books of the 'De Civitate Dei.' Following S. Augustine, Otto definitely rejects the Chiliastic doctrine, that our Lord will return for a terrestrial millennium and reign visibly in any sense in which He is not now reigning. This work alone is evidence of the way in which the great Christian Commonwealth can be regarded alike as Empire and Church, and is thought of as *Civitas Dei.*

Let us go forward a century. In S. Thomas Aquinas the

mediæval world has its most authoritative statement, just as Dante gave it its imaginative symbol The ordered intelligence of S. Thomas was different in the extreme from the highly emotional and stormy intellect of S. Augustine. In the writings of S. Thomas we have a minutely articulated system of mediæval thought as it had come to be in the day of the supreme achievements of the Papacy. Born ten years after the death of Innocent III, S. Thomas lived through most of the latter phases of the Hohenstauffen struggle, more especially the Council of Lyons and the despotism of the 'stupor mundi et immutator mirabilis ' Frederic II. We do well to take him as the central point for the understanding of mediæval thought.

S. Thomas's system of politics is expressed in several places. First there is the commentary on Aristotle's 'Politics.' With that we are not concerned in this connection. There is the not inconsiderable discussion of fundamentals in politics in the 'Summa Theologica,' ii. 2, qq. 90-109, and also in certain other passages of the same work anent heretics, and so forth. Lastly we have the little treatise 'De Regimine Principum.' Of this only the first book and four chapters of the second are written by S. Thomas. The rest is by Ptolemy of Lucca.

S. Thomas has been called the first Whig. His discussion of forms of government follows on Aristotle's. Of all that I make abstraction to-day. When you study him in detail you see that he develops his system in dependence on three main authorities—Scripture, Aristotle, and Augustine. I do not know how many times S. Augustine is cited in the 'Summa,' but I should suppose it must be quoted thousands of times. In the parts which deal with politics, we find a great deal of dependence upon him. We do not hear of the doctrine of the two cities, for the obvious reason that it was no longer held to fit, now that the kingdom of this world had become the kingdom of our God and His Christ: and the other use of the terms (that maintained by Otto), to denote merely the elect and the reprobate, does not, strictly speaking, concern politics.

S. Thomas quotes most from S. Augustine's 'De Libero Arbitrio,' but we have important arguments drawn from the 'De Civitate Dei.' He makes much use of that definition—the Ciceronian—

which makes justice the essence of a State. In the passage which justifies war (ii. 2, q. 40, 1) no fewer than eight passages are adduced. Further on, in article 3, he argues, from Augustine's words in the ' De Civitate Dei,' that stratagems in warfare are legitimate. S. Thomas discusses whether it be right to carry the doctrine of the Christianity of the State so far as to make vice equivalent to crime. This he decides in the negative. He was too wise to want a Puritan tyranny. He does this on grounds derived entirely from S. Augustine. At the same time he disclaims any idea of treating Augustine as an infallible guide. On the treatment of heretics he bases his argument for persecution upon three passages of S. Augustine. Like Augustine also he condemns compulsion of the heathen. He even goes so far as to say that a Christian governor would be right to tolerate heathen ceremonies. A heretic or schismatic is an erring and rebellious child, and is therefore to be corrected. Quite other is the case of the Jew or the Pagan. His treatment of neighbours' lives and property is in line with S. Augustine, especially the remarkable passages in which he defends the social and industrial legislation of the Mosaic system, on the ground that it is all based on the idea of fellowship.

Further evidence is to be found in the 'De Regimine Principum.' In treatment and manner it is unlike S. Augustine. But we find more than one reference to the 'De Civitate Dei,' especially the reproduction of the Mirror of Princes. Even more relevant is the argument from ends. The true end and reward of a godly prince must be beyond this life. We have arguments much the same as those of S. Augustine, only applied rather to the prince than the *respublica.* In I, 14 there is a long and elaborate argument to show that the end of a well-governed commonwealth must be virtuous life, which leads to the fruition of God. Since the lord of the ultimate end must obviously direct those who are concerned only with subordinate ends, the Roman pontiff must have the ultimate authority over Christian kings, just as among the ancient Gauls the Druids held the control.

It is interesting, and for our purpose not impertinent, to go on with the book and consider the later parts written by Ptolemy of Lucca. They are fair evidence of the mediæval ideals and were written not much later. Here we have a direct and continuous dependence on the 'De Civitate Dei.' It is not merely a question of the influence of ideas, but of the following of the book. References to it are numerous. Many arguments are drawn from it. S. Augustine is the writer's acknowledged authority for the claim that the Romans were entrusted with the dominion of the world as a reward for their virtue; and Christians are bidden to imitate this self-sacrifice. From S. Augustine is cited the interpretation of the words about the image and superscription of Cæsar; that the image of Cæsar was (as it were) the image of God. Ptolemy accepts Augustine's account of the difference between despotic and properly political power, arguing that the former would never have been known but for sin. The writer seems to have had the aim of harmonising Aristotle and Augustine. We need not follow him in his description of the Empire or in his criticism of ancient constitutions. All that we need observe is this, that in this book, which is a moderate but definite expression of the hierarchical theory of the State, we have ample evidence that the influence of S. Augustine was not merely an universally pervading force in the Middle Ages, but was consciously adopted and felt.

Towards the close of the Middle Ages we can still trace the direct influence of S. Augustine in political thought. One writer (I think a Frenchman) arguing in favour of national States, at a time when the imperial authority was no more than a name, at least in France, makes free use of the passage in the 'De Civitate Dei' which maintains the value of a multitude of small societies.

Dante's 'De Monarchia' is the best known, as it is the most impressive, of the accounts of the Holy Roman Empire. It is, as you know, Ghibelline, *i.e.* Imperialist, and is designed to show that the Emperor holds his sceptre by grace of God immediately, not mediately through the Pope. The claim was not new. Henry IV made it against Hildebrand. So also did the Hohenstauffen. Dante's grandiose conception is still that of the mediæval unity—a great world Church-State. I do not think that the book as a whole can be said to depend on S. Augustine. But it is hardly possible not to suspect that the second book did owe much to the 'De Civitate Dei.' In that book Dante proves that the Empire of the world was given to the

Romans for all time, as a reward of virtue. It is noticeable that Dante quotes the 'De Civitate Dei' once.

Very interesting is the book ' On the Origin and Progress of the Roman Empire,' from which a quotation has already been made. It is by Engelbert, Abbot of Admont, in Austria.[8] The writer founds his argument to a large extent on the 'De Civitate Dei.' Most of the book is little more than a comment on this. It was written at the time (1310) of the last strictly mediæval revival of the Empire under Henry of Luxemburg, and after the final defeat of the Hohenstauffen, *i.e.* about the same time as Dante's book. The writer had to face the existing conditions, with the *de facto* independence of France. Therefore he takes into account S. Augustine's view that the world would fare better under a number of independent communities, joined in one bond of harmony and respecting each other. This he counters in the following argument Such, he says, is the mutual jealousy between nations that no such harmony is to be looked for. The only chance of peace is for the world to become one State. The argument has reference mainly to Catholic Christendom in the West. One remarkable passage takes into account the existence of non-Christian States. They, he says, are equally bound by national law and must recognise the principle of justice which is *suum cuique tribuere*. In other words the principle at the bottom of international amity is seen to be the maxim to love one another, which is supposed to govern the human race. This is not far from the maxim of William of Ockham, which was a little later, that all men compose one society. What for our purpose is most noteworthy is the author's view, that Christianity has now become the law of the greater part of the world, and a Christian Empire is therefore the ideal.

One most interesting passage is of prophetic import. Arguing, as Engelbert did, in favour of the imperial ideal at a time when the most progressive States of Europe had freed themselves and the national monarchies were being consolidated, he declares that the unity of the Holy Roman Empire is two-fold, both secular and ecclesiastical, and that if the nations withdraw themselves from recognition of the Emperor, it will not be long before they throw off allegiance to the Pope.

97

Even more prophetic are the writings of Wyclif. Wyclif is enormously dependent on S. Augustine. He develops that other side in Augustine's conception of the Church which was at times conveniently ignored by the clericalists—that which insists on its primary application to the elect and no one else. He does this with conscious use of S. Augustine. This leads straight to the doctrine of the Invisible Church.

Finally, he uses S. Augustine to support his radical Erastianism. From him he develops the doctrine that the clergy must always be subordinate to the civil power, for royalty represents the fatherhood of God and the priesthood the sonship. He cites S. Augustine in regard to the image and superscription of Cæsar. Wyclif was the most thoroughgoing Erastian who ever lived. He wrote after Marsilius of Padua, and was probably influenced by the 'Defensor Pacis' with its programme of democratic Erastianism. Most of Wyclif's works are a plea for the disendowment of the Church. The 'De Dominio Civili' is not mainly a treatise on politics, as its name might seem to imply. It is concerned with property, and especially with corporate property. Wyclif wants the Church to be disendowed. Then, he says, the lords, having more lands, will have less motive to oppress the poor. In the 'Speculum Militantis Ecclesiae' he treats of the Church as equivalent to the commonwealth, and declares that it consists of the lords, the clergy and the labouring classes![9] His doctrine of dominion founded on grace is intended to argue that property has duties as well as rights, i.e. that the right of private property is not absolute. That indeed was the view of S. Thomas and S. Augustine. It was the Roman pagan conception of absolute property that triumphed at the close of the Middle Ages. This idea, which is the foundation of modern capitalism, led at the time to further attempts to depress the peasants into slavery. It has been fraught with a thousand evils, from which even now the world is slowly and with many struggles trying to recover. The 'reception,' as it is called, of Roman Law in 1495 in Germany may be taken as the date when the Middle Ages came to an end and the Roman ideas of property had conquered the West.

The great mediæval unity was always largely an ideal. Still it was the ideal. It was a unity of religion, of government, of economics, of morals, of social life and of outward culture. This unity, if not determined by S. Augustine, owed much to his influence. It was not the direct or intended result of his writing. He spoke, indeed, of things not being so bad as people thought, of a possible revival of the Roman power. For this he has been blamed. It is said he showed lack of prescience. But was it so? The actual Roman Empire lasted in the West for more than half a century after S. Augustine's death. Then came the Ostrogothic kingdom of Theodoric. That too vanished. Justinian's conquest is not to be ignored. Why should it be?

Augustine did not foresee the Holy Roman Empire of the German people, or the cry of Gerbert to Otto III, 'Nostrum, nostrum est imperium Romanum' Yet such a phrase may be held to have justified his words. For it was the Roman ideal that stood for peace and culture in those troublous times.

Easier is it to trace this influence in the doctrine of the whole world as the *Civitas Dei,* connecting this with S. Augustine's undoubted belief in the unity and universal mission of the Church, and his assimilation of it to a society.

Easier still is it to trace his influence in the otherworldly reference which lay behind all mediæval developments, in the growth of Western monasticism with its characteristic qualities, with the widespread acceptance of his principle of property.

Some would trace to S. Augustine the whole development of the Papal power. This was hardly a legitimate development, but not at all impossible.

Clearly we cannot understand the Middle Ages on this political and social side without Augustine. He it is who helped much to make the Western world compact.

Notes to Lecture V

[1] *De ortu progressu et fine Romani imperii* in Goldast, *Politico,* (Frankfurt, 1614), pp. 754—773.

[2] For 'Erastus' see the essay appended to 'Divine Right of Kings' (and edition, 1914), pp. 293 and ff; for 'Respublica Christiana,' see 'Churches in the Modern State,' Appendix I, pp. 175 and ff.

[3] C. Mirbt, *Die Stellung Augustins in der Publicistik des Gregorianischen Kirchenstreits* (Leipzig, 1888), p. 111.

'In der Erorterung fast aller Fragen, welche die Controverslitteratur zu behandehi hatte, zeigt sich der Einfluss Augustins; besonders: in der Lehre von der Kirche, in der Erorterung des Verhaltnisses von Kirche und Staat, in der Besprechung der Excommunication, in dem Streit iiber die Objectivitat der Sakramente.'

[4] *Cf.* the following letter of Henry IV in 1073. Jaffé, *Bibl. Rer. Germ,* ii (*Monumenta Gregoriana*), p. 46.

'Cum enim regnum et sacerdotium ut in Christo rite administrata subsistant, vicaria sui ope semper indigeant, oportet nimirum, domine mi et pater amantissime, quatinus ab invicem minime dissentiant.verum potius Christi glutino conjunctissima indissolubiliter sibi cohaereant.'

[5] Walram of Naumburg, *De Unitate Ecclesie conseruanda,* i. 17, in *Libelli de lite* (*Mon. Germ. Hist.*), ii. pp. 184 and ff.

[6] Gregory, *Reg.* viii. 21. Migne, *P.L.,* cxlviii. 596, 598.

[7] Humbertus, *Adv. Simoniacos,iii.* 29, in Martène, *Thes.* v. 819 *sq.*

'Quis fidelium dubitare jam poterit Spiritum sanctum . . . totam replere ecclesiam, ut pro qualitate ministrorum et rerum eius singula quae illi connectuntur et debentur sanctificet? Est enim *clericalis or do in ecclesia praecipuus* tanquam in capite oculi. . .

. Est et laicolis potestas tanquam pectus et brachia ad obediendum et defendendum ecclesiam valida et exerta. Est deinde vulgus tanquam inferiora vel extrema membra ecclesiasticis et saecularibus potestatibus pariter subditum et pernecessarium.'

[8] See note 1.

[9] Compare also Wyclif, *De Officio Regis,* 58, 59.

'Necesse est esse tres hierarchias in regno quae omnes unam personam unicordem constituant, scilicet sacerdotes vel oratores, seculares dominos vel defensores, et plebeos vel laboratores.'

THE 'DE CIVITATE DEI'
IN LATER DAYS

THE mediæval unity was the grandest attempt in human history to base the structure of institutions upon righteousness, political, social and economic, no less than religious. When this unity broke up, a new world—as Luther said—came into being. It might seem as though the ideals connected with the mediæval projection of the *Civitas Dei* were gone beyond recall. That is true only partially. The break up of the ancient order did destroy this idea for Europe as a whole. Take such works as the 'Utopia' of Sir Thomas More and the 'Il Principe' of Macchiavelli. We can see how men's dreams were changed no less than the facts. The Renaissance appeared to have put an end to all such hopes as those which animated S. Thomas.

Macchiavelli's remorseless study of the facts of the inter-state scramble in Italy is more remarkable for what it leaves out than for what it puts in. The conception of natural law has vanished. The passion of nationality furnishes the one ideal. In the moving and pathetic eloquence of the last chapter he cries for a saviour, who shall do for distressed Italy what other saviours have done for their people.

'If, as I said, in order to show the valour of Moses it was necessary for the people of Israel to be enslaved in Egypt; and, for the magnanimity of Cyrus to be seen, it was needful for the Persians to be oppressed by the Medes; and, to illustrate the excellence of Theseus, the Athenians had to be dispersed: so now, for the virtue of an Italian spirit to be seen, it was needful that Italy should be reduced to the state in which she now is, and to be more enslaved than were the Hebrews, more oppressed than the Persians, more scattered than the Athenians, without head, without order beaten, dispirited, lacerated, hunted, and in fact enduring every kind of ruin.'

Nothing can be nobler than Macchiavelli's desire for a redeemer of his people. But of justice, whether in the internal government or in the external relations of a people, he took no thought. Everything is reason of state.

Savonarola's ideal for Florence, to be a godfearing city with a true democracy, had been given a trial. It had failed. With this failure, so far as the Italian States were concerned, there disappeared all efforts at ideal politics, until in the nineteenth century Macchiavelli's ideals triumphed by Macchiavelli's own methods. Italy became united under the headship of Victor Emmanuel and the astute diplomacy of Cavour. There was a man after Macchiavelli's heart. He had his reward.

In Europe as a whole the Reformation destroyed the last hopes of a united Christendom. The 'Balance of Power' became the guiding-star of statesmen. From the League of Cambrai to the Partition of Poland was a natural development. We too have seen it even go further. Acton said ' Calvin preached, and Bellarmin lectured, but Macchiavelli reigned.' Here, however, a faint shadow of the old ideal can be discerned in the ideas and principles which underlay modern International Law.

In regard to both these developments it is possible to trace the influence, if not the direct ancestry of ideas, to S. Augustine.

It has been thought that the second definition of a commonwealth in the ' De Civitate Dei,' that in which the ideas of justice and religion do not appear, may have had something to do with the development of the non-moral doctrine of the State. It is doubtful how far this can be proved. This much is clear. Augustine emphasised the aim of the terrene State as being earthly peace and no more. This limitation has much to do with the rapidly developing theory of the secular State. That was developed largely by the Jesuits, in order the better to exalt the Church, the *Respublica Christiana.* Jesuit writers and others on that side developed frankly a doctrine of the civil

State as being purely secular and having no ends that were not material. It can have to do with higher ideals only in so far as it is directed to these ends by the supreme religious guide. That is the principle of Bellarmin developed frankly and without disguise. This is different from the principles of writers like Augustinus Triumphus at the end of the Middle Ages, or of Bozius in the sixteenth century. These definitely make the whole world a single State, of which the Pope as 'King of Kings and Lord of Lords' is head. Bellarmin's doctrine of the indirect power of the Papacy allows to the civil State a being and purpose of its own. On one side it is frankly secular. The State of the Jesuits, when once it threw off its ecclesiastical tutelage, would be more, not less, indifferent in matters of religion—more also than was the old pagan State.

The distinction on which all this argument depends unfortunately comes through S. Augustine. We saw that he was not always thinking of politics. Yet it remains true that the whole conception of the State as *Civitas terrena* is precisely what enabled the Jesuits to set up their doctrine of the civil State. Since also it virtually coincided with the doctrine of pure politics, which emerged at the Renaissance, it helped to produce our general modern notions.

On the other hand the influence of Augustine on the growth of International Law is certain. That he laid down principles which might prove fruitful, if they were needed, cannot be denied. The conception of a world of equal States living in harmony and exchanging mutual services we owe to his mind, expressed in the passage about a world consisting of small States We cannot say that the founders of International Law depended upon S. Augustine. In Albericus Gentilis, 'De Jure Belli,' there are no citations from the 'De Civitate Dei.' In the great work of Grotius, 'De Jure Belli et Pads,' Augustine is frequently cited. This need not mean much. Here and there important arguments are based on these quotations. Yet so many authorities are adduced that it is hard to attribute priority to any single one. The avowed doctrine of Grotius is Natural Law. Certainly that is in S. Augustine, but Grotius did not take it from him. Still the general conceptions which are to be found in the ' De Civitate Dei,' of the mitigation of warfare through Christianity, of the sense of a common bond between nations, the insistence upon justice, the bitter condemnation of a policy of mere conquest—all these were among the many influences that helped to keep alive some flickering brands of Christendom, implying something better than the 'law of the beasts.' I am not certain that we can say more. The great ideal of a world ruled by justice had gone. If, however, the nations, now definitely recognised as sovereign and independent, should ever come to concord, they might point to the passage of which I have so often spoken, as laying down the ideal of world-politics in a body of States independent but mutually concordant.

So much for Christendom and the great State. When we come to reduce the scale, the story is different. In the narrower field of compact territorial sovereignty, governments were not necessarily irresponsive to the same ideals that we saw embodied in the Holy Roman Empire. Moreover, during the long period of the wars of religion until at least 1609, when the Dutch won their long truce, and in a less degree until 1648, when absolute differences of religion were guaranteed at the Peace of Westphalia, the idea of some sort of Christendom survived. The State, as conceived by the Renaissance, the embodiment of power and nothing but power, did not triumph finally, except later on in Prussia. That was prevented by the Reformation, with its emphasis on theocratic and scriptural ideas of government.

In the first place, the concentrated territorialism of the new States in Germany made the unity of religion with them a feasible aim—a Lutheran could leave a Calvinist State and live elsewhere still under the same 'Kultur.' So much so that one elector could say that 'his subjects' consciences belonged to him.' What triumphed everywhere was Erastianism—the lay power in a Christian State ruling over the clerical. Luther did not desire a State religiously heterogeneous. He did not desire a State founded on power alone. Luther and Melanchthon desired to transfer to civic and family life all the consecration of aim associated heretofore with monastic devotion. Erastus himself declared that he was considering the case of a State in which one religion and one only was tolerated, and that the true one. The control of the inner life of the Church by a Parliament, which might be composed of 'Jews, Turks, infidels and heretics,' was the last thing that Erastus contemplated. What he desired was to take all coercive authority out of the hands of the clergy, and transfer it to the civil magistrate. Stubbs says of Henry VIII 'that he would be the Pope, the whole Pope and something more than the Pope,' referring to the jurisdiction. The movement was a layman's movement, not in itself anti-religious. Its ideal is 'the godly prince.' Its State is a commonwealth in which Christ is King, no whit less than was the mediæval theocracy. All through the period of the Reformation this ideal expresses itself.

With this expression there grew a more explicit recognition of the Commonwealth and the Church as two aspects of the same society. This doctrine was not confined to men of any especial opinion. It is the doctrine of Luther and Musculus and of John Knox but also of Whitgift and Laud and the more extreme Gallican lawyers in France, but not of Bossuet. We in England have this doctrine enshrined for ever by the serene and gracious intelligence of Hooker. Nothing could be clearer than his statement:

'When we oppose the Church, therefore, and the Commonwealth in a Christian society, we mean by the Commonwealth that society with relation unto all the public affairs thereof, only the matter of true religion excepted; by the Church the same society with only reference unto the matter of true religion, without any other affairs besides; when that society which is both a Church and a Commonwealth doth flourish in these things which belong to it as a Commonwealth, we then say the Commonwealth doth flourish; when in the things which concern it as a Church, the Church doth flourish; when in both, then the Church and the Commonwealth flourish together,' (Hooker, *Ecclesiastical Polity*, viii. 15 ; *Works,* iii. 420.)

The opposite doctrine of the two kingdoms, as found in Hooker's adversary, Thomas Cartwright, is greeted by Whitgift with surprise as a strange monstrous birth. This doctrine, that of Church and State as two distinct societies, was developed by Huguenots in France, by Independents like Robert Browne in his treatise 'Reformation without tarrying for any' (*any* meaning

106

the civil magistrate), but above all by the second generation of Presbyterians. It might be alleged by the Presbyterians that their doctrine was more akin to S. Augustine than that of the Middle Ages. No more than S. Augustine did the Presbyterians leave the State free in the interests of religion, but demanded that the Prince should use force to direct men for their good. The famous words of

Andrew Melville to James I in 1606 are a classical expression of it.

It was, however, the earlier doctrine that long ruled— the conception of the State as in sort a Church—inside a compact unitary State. The argument for unity which in the Middle Ages had been employed partly on behalf of the Emperor, but more effectively on that of the Pope, could now be made the ground for treating the civil power as 'over all persons and in all causes supreme.' This principle of religious unity as a foundation of the Commonwealth and the only possible source of justice, was proclaimed by people of widely different opinions. In France we have the *une loi, un roi, une foi* of pamphleteers like Louis d'Orléans. This cry produced the 'conversion' of Henri Quatre, and ultimately the revocation of the Edict of Nantes, parallel with the assertion of extreme royalism in the Gallican Articles of 1682 and the threat to break off from Rome. On the other side we have Erastus proclaiming that there could be no coercive authority in the spiritual power, hinting that if necessary the prince could teach and administer the sacraments, developing into the doctrine of 'the Lord's Anointed' as a *persona mixta,* partly lay, partly ecclesiastical. A little later we see it expressed in the absolutism of Hobbes; and symbolised on his famous frontispiece. On the largest scale we see Hooker applying it to a nation-state. But it is not confined to that. Anabaptists are often treated as mere anarchists. That is only one side of them. The constructive governing side was shown in the attempt to secure a State inspired in every detail by Christian principles. Knipperdolling, the King, as he was called, of Münster, put this into practice. It is adumbrated in the 'Restitution' of Rothmann, who argues against the Chiliasts and in favour of a Kingdom of Christ on earth now, thus recalling S. Augustine.

107

Calvin at Geneva and the Puritan polities illustrate the same principle. The reign of the saints, so called, was but the counterpart, on the narrower scale, of the doctrine of the rule of Christ in a truly just republic— of that rule which the Canonists and Ultramontanes gave to the Pope.

Let us take a literary expression of this. 'Nova Solyma,' which appeared in 1648, is an attempt to imagine the city of God upon earth, 'to build Jerusalem,' as the name implies. It is a work of amazing interest both for its educational and political ideals. Despite much that was irritating in his manner, Mr. Begley, who published a translation in 1902, has done service in recalling this didactic romance from limbo. Let me quote from an article in the *Church Quarterly* which I wrote on the topic in the following year.

'Puritanism, like nearly all ascetic ideals, had in it a strong Manichean bias. We know it chiefly by its enmities. It was active for destruction. It destroyed the monarchy, the aristocracy, and finally the representative system. It abolished the drama, it proscribed the Liturgy, it persecuted the bishops, it knocked down statues, overturned altars and shattered windows. It first abolished tyranny and then destroyed liberty and finally completed its career of devastation by giving the *coup de grâce* to itself. Few movements have been to all appearances more uniform in their destructive tendencies than was English political Puritanism. But it is no more right to judge Puritanism by its antipathies than it is Christianity. . . . It is the constructive side of Puritanism that "Nova Solyma" expresses. . . .

'Puritanism at its best was constructive. Starting from the conception, made familiar to us all by Mr. James, of the twice-born soul, it desired to see a new "city of God" upon earth, in which, with whatever latitude for political and natural differences, the life of the Christian should be properly trained and guarded by a State directed by religious principles and acting solely from the highest aims. . . .

'This ideal of a Christian State in accordance with Puritan principles is the whole purpose of "Nova Solyma." . . . It is the

108

XVIIth Century *Civitas Dei,* as indeed its name implies. . . . Though Puritanism as a politico-religious party was not long in the ascendant, many of its governing ideas found their way into the more serious-minded of all classes, and have had a profound effect upon the national character. These or some of them will be found in "Nova Solyma," where we can learn that the Puritan was no Little Englander, no mere ascetic, no opponent of war, or hunting, or reading as such; but that his ideal was a State governed on principles of righteousness, training its members—body, mind, and spirit—in all the faculties and sentiments which may minister to the efficiency and energy appropriate to the conduct of a Christian member of an orderly and self-controlling society. Religion since the Reformation, said Sir A. F. Hort, has been departmental, and given up the aim of controlling the whole of human life in the way that mediæval Catholicism attempted. This is unfortunately to a certain extent true, but was not so always or in aim ; and such books as "Nova Solyma" are the proof of a broader ideal.' (*C.Q.R.,* lvii. No. 113, Oct. 1903, 125-130.)

That work is English. Take one which is not. Johann Valentin Andreae in 'Christianopolis' affords a similar illustration.[1] Here, too, the main interest of the whole is in its ideals of education. But it is on a smaller scale and in every way inferior to ' Nova Solyma.' Both of them show how deeply men's imaginations were affected by the doctrine of an ideal Christian Commonwealth.

Let us now take instances from men of opposite Political sympathies. The doctrine of the 'Divine Right of Kings,' on its religious as distinct from its legal and historical side, is an expression of the notion that the civil State ought to be a commonwealth of Christians, the *Civitas Dei.* It is this half-romantic, half-sacramental doctrine which consecrated to many the cause of the Stuarts. This religious side of the doctrine was as a rule stronger in England than in France.

Yet Bossuet's 'Politique Tirée de l'Ecriture Sainte' is a good illustration of it. Bossuet prided himself on this dull work which looked towards the past, although it must be admitted that Bossuet never merged the Church in the State, but always regarded them as two societies. It is well to take this work as an illustration. With the beginning of the eighteenth century the end had come, so far as this country was concerned. The Nonjuring schism had considerable importance It developed strongly in the minds of men like William Law (in his letters to Hoadly) the doctrine of the Church, as a society in itself distinct from the State, though it might be composed of the same persons. Each body was, in the later phrase of Leo XIII, a *societas genere et jure perfecta.* The Bangorian controversy which was aroused by Hoadly's sermon 'The Kingdom of Christ,' showed the same notion in the religious sphere. Hoadly was dominated by the ancient notion which made the Church co-extensive with the nation; and therefore desired the comprehension within it of anybody and everybody. Sherlock and his other opponents asserted the distinctness and historic independence of the Church, and the incompetence of the civil power to control it. This tendency had been increased by other causes. The Toleration Act and the Union with Scotland destroyed the notion of a uniform religious State. True it left some basis, for the Toleration Act stopped short of Unitarianism or the Papacy, and the Scots refused to tolerate episcopacy. But now the Kingdom, united as never before, was not even professedly uniform in religion. It boasted two different established churches. Naturally, this led to a resuscitation, even among establishment Divines, of the doctrine of the two Societies.

Warburton's 'Alliance between Church and State' is a better book than many people think. It lays down that the two bodies are entirely distinct in nature, though they may be composed of the same individuals. But the State establishes a Church from a utilitarian, not from a religious motive. It is not the business of the State to seek the truth, but merely to take the religion of the majority of its members and establish that. As the eighteenth and nineteenth centuries proceeded, the old Augustinian doctrine of a Christian Church-State prevailing in the Middle Ages, and through the Reformation, gradually disappeared. Toleration gave way to complete civil rights for Dissenters, Roman Catholics, Jews, and finally Atheists. It has been recently decided in the Courts that a bequest to a Free Thinking Association was legal. Religious heterogeneity is recognised as a principle of the modern State. In Mr. Gladstone's early book, ' The State in its Relations with the Church,' we find a last echo of the old view. But he does not contemplate, like Hooker, a single society. Rather, he treats the Church as the conscience of the State, and deprecates on that ground the admission of the Jews to full political rights.

The notion of a theocracy has more and more receded from discussions on general politics. The notion of the principles of Christian ethics—*i.e.* the golden rule, which is held by many non-Christians on different grounds —as the governing doctrine of political and social justice, has tended to increase in importance. Not merely Christian socialism, but many more general doctrines of humanity, are content to argue that (in this sense) the world is or ought to be Christian, and its legislation ought to be framed according to the Jewish-Christian rule of fraternity. This tendency has been enhanced by the war. Many who before regarded Christianity as an effete system of impossible dogmas awakened to find that the real difference between the belligerents was nothing less than the prevalence of certain ethical ideals, of which the most eminent if not the only expression was the Christian system. Reconstruction,

it is alleged, in order to be stable, must follow these lines— whether applied to Europe as a whole in the relations between States, or to the domestic economy of peoples, or to the relations of classes. As the doctrine of absolute state-sovereignty is criticised, so also is the companion doctrine of absolute rights in private property. Neither of these criticisms is new, even in modern times. Both have been rendered more acute by the war, *i.e.* the ideal of a State is more and more seen to be dependent on justice.

Only, as S. Augustine failed to see, justice in politics and in social economy has reference only to those ideals of *cuique suum tribuere* and the Golden Rule, which are not necessarily in fact bound up with religion. Men can unite in those, who yet differ *in toto* on the theological foundation. In this sense indeed it may be natural to look forward to a Christian State; but certainly it is neither natural nor wise to do so in the sense of a State which promulgates the Christian religion and none other.

Consequently, while legislation or custom may well be pressed on the ground of its accordance with Christian principles, so far as they are confined to the social doctrine, it is impolitic and even wrong to condemn or promote legislation on the ground that it conflicts with the law of the Christian Church. That is to attempt to make what is true only of one society govern the whole.

To sum up, with the Renaissance the secular or pagan State tended to become the ideal. This effect was counteracted by the Reformation. Yet that destroyed the ancient unity of Western Christendom and made impossible the ideal of the Holy Roman Empire, of a single Catholic Commonwealth of princes and lords and peoples, a unity of all culture. Vestiges of this lingered on and helped towards the beginning of modern International Law. On the smaller scale of the separate State, the effect of the Reformation was different. It tightened instead of loosening all those ties that made for a concentrated unitary State. So much so, that it is even now but slowly and with infinite reluctance that political problems can be discussed on any other basis. For the more part within that State it shifted the balance of power from the clergy to the laity, the Church to the State, the Pope to the King. If we recognise that change, we can say that the ideal of a uniform Christian commonwealth was as real to Hooker as it was to Alfred the Great. This was the aim of the great national States like England and France, of the smaller territorial sovereignties in Germany, with their maxim *cujus regio ejus religio,* and even of bodies like the Anabaptists and Pilgrim Fathers, as soon as they obtained rule. We see this expressed on the grand scale by Hooker and Whitgift, on the smaller scale by Rothmann and 'Nova Solyma.' In some of the arguments adduced in favour of established churches, and in certain vague appeals to Christian principles, it can be discerned in our own days, and can be traced right back to S. Augustine. On the whole, however, religious heterogeneity is recognised as a fundamental part of the modern State, but in regard to certain fundamental ethical principles of neighbourliness, mutual love and so forth, Christian morals (as apart from any kind of theology) are increasingly recognised as integral to a just and even to a stable organisation of life.

On the other hand, the development of the secular, this-worldly theory of the State, whether by Jesuits or Presbyterians in their own interest, owes much to the other and more commonly neglected side of S. Augustine—that in which he openly discarded the principles of religion in the idea of a commonwealth. The sharp distinction between secular and sacred, holy and profane, which ruled historical writing until recently, though not introduced, was enormously strengthened by S. Augustine.

The problem which S. Augustine discussed in this book is fundamental, nor has it ever been finally resolved. It is a conflict not primarily between two polities. To make it that, is to externalise it and to make it relatively superficial, deep down in history though even that goes. Rather the conflict is one between two religions— Christianity and Paganism. That is S. Augustine's primary and predominating thought. It never leaves him. These two religions are conceived as the binding force of two societies, the expression of two opposing passions: *Fecerunt itaque civitates duas amores duo*— the passion for God and the passion for self. That is the direction alike of angelic and human wills, which makes the whole time-process since the fall of Lucifer a drama of eternal tragedy, and conditions the Redemption. If we seek to understand S. Augustine mainly by the outcome to which his system led in history, we shall do wrong. Rather we must seek to understand that by the deeper antagonism—between the other-worldly and the this-worldly reference of all institutions. This we shall realise better by a more intimate personal knowledge of the most intimate and personal of all divines until John Henry Newman. In Augustine there were struggling two men, like Esau and Jacob in the womb of Rebecca. There was Augustine of Thagaste, of Madaura, of Carthage, of Rome, of Milan, the brilliant boy, the splendid and expansive youthful leader, 'skilled in all the wisdom of the Egyptians,' possessed of the antique culture, rhetorical, dialectic, Roman— the man of the world, the developed humanist with enough tincture of Platonism to gild the humanism; and there is the Augustine of the 'Confessions,' of the 'Sermons,' of the 'De Civitate,' the monk, the ascetic, the other-worldly preacher, the biblical expositor, the mortified priest. These two beings struggle for ever within him, the natural man filled with the sense of beauty and the joy of living, expansive, passionate, artful—and the supernatural Christian fleeing from the world, shunning it, burning what he adored, and adoring what he burnt, celibate and (at times) almost anti-social.

This book itself is too great to be consistent. We can see in it traces of this ceaseless conflict. The otherworldly aim is predominant, the annihilation of all earthly values in comparison with the *summum bonum*.

But evidences, we have noted, remain of the humane, social, cultured ideal. The conflict is eternal in human life. No change of religion will put a term to it. Not even as some think, as I suppose Augustine thought, the abolition of all eternal values. On the one hand is the world, the present, the course of life, the immediate 'nice things'; and on the other the Eternal, the far-off, the spiritual city, the altar of sacrifice, the chalice of suffering—each calls us, each finds response in our nature. How can this problem be resolved? One way is by complete world-flight, the extreme of asceticism, *i.e.* asceticism not as discipline but as self-annihilation, or, as seen in the sphere of institutions, in the utter subjection of the city of this world to the rule of those who speak in the name of the Eternal. On the other is the pagan solution, frankly materialistic, developing on its better side a grand picture of human society, and a high development of all human arts, but ruling out as irrelevant all interests that look beyond. Neither by itself can satisfy.

The real change in S. Augustine took place when he was converted to Platonism by reading Cicero's 'Hortensius' and not in the later well-known scene in the garden at Milan. From that first moment related in the 'Confessions' he had the nostalgia of the infinite, and all earthly goods were annihilated to his restless spirit. The charge brought by Nietzsche against Plato that he did the real damage, preparatory to Christianity, by setting up the doctrine of another world is true.

Perhaps it is this which makes Augustine's apologetic more impressive on the general theistic, than it is on its distinctively Christian, side.

114

Yet that fact suggests the solution. Plato, and still more the Neo-Platonists, showed that a mere humanistic culture is bankrupt at the last, for man's heart is restless until he find God. Even humanism as an ideal cannot be carried out without an infusion of the otherworldly principle—present pleasure must be given up for future bliss even by an Alexander.

Augustine calls attention to this. The Romans, he said, were moved by earthly motives of ambition, no more. To that end they were prodigal of sacrifice. Christians for their end, which is so much higher, would do well if they were to learn the devotion to the heavenly *patria* which the Romans gave to an earthly one. In other words, the Roman State, the earthly aim, could not be maintained except by sacrifice. True, the sacrifice is for an end of this world alone. Yet it is equally sacrifice of the immediate for a far-off end, for an individual and even for a community like Saguntum it means the surrender of life itself for the good of the whole. What makes this possible?

Even earthly ambitions apart from the State, even sheer individualism, can make no progress without sacrifice and what Christians call the Cross. Any successful merchant knows that. Even the hardest voluptuary must postpone immediate goods—in the Christian phrase, must die to live—and take risks, or he will not fulfil the demands of his passions.

Thus then the edifce of humane culture cannot but rest its foundations on the principle of the Cross, and also upon social and communal interdependence. ' Man cannot live for himself alone.' Yet this principle has in many cases no meaning and no appeal to the individual, if there be no world beyond.

Take the other side. Sheer world-flight is not possible. The extremest ascetic—S. Simon on his pillar—must be fed. In the 'De Opere Monachorum S. Augustine points this out.[2] It is all very well, he says, for people to say that a man ought to be entirely occupied with the things of God, and therefore need do no labour. This cannot be. The dinner must be cooked. Some manual work is a necessity in any self-sufficing society. Therefore it cannot be contrary to true monastic life to do some secular work.

115

Besides, whether for the selfish end which we considered above, or for the religious, sheer individualism would be the final abutment of either, world-flight or world-acceptance, taken by itself. Sheer individualism is literally unthinkable. A selfish man of culture needs the help of society at every turn. A world-renouncing monk cannot do without security. Social and communal activities are of the essence of human life, for no one can dispense with them. If they are, then sacrifice of what we want, even, on occasion, of life itself, becomes a necessity at times, a fact of which to-day we have lurid evidence. Nor in the long run can such sacrifice be justified to the individual apart from an other-worldly aim. The goods of human sacrifice are real goods. But just as the individual is driven to the larger life of the community by the natural fact of the family, so human society and all human culture is possible only by the ultimate recognition of the eternal goal. Otherwise there will come the decadence, such as overcame Greece and Rome and the Renaissance. That is the lesson of the 'De Civitate Dei.' Our ideals of beauty must be rooted in the hope of eternal life—earthly glories are symbols and sacraments—if they be not evil; for 'God created man to be immortal and made him an image of his own eternity,' or in his own words: 'Thou hast made us for thyself, and our heart is restless until it find thee.'

Notes to Lecture VI

[1] *Christianopolis,* trs. by Dr. F. E. Held (Oxford University Press, New York, 1916).

[2] 'De opere monachorum,' *C.* xvii.

'Quid enim agant qui operari corporaliter nolunt, cui rei vacent scire desidero. Orationibus inquiunt et psalmis et lectioni et verbo dei. Sancta plane vita, et Christi suauitate laudabilis. Sed si ab his auocandi non sumus, nee manducandum est, nee ipsae escae quotidie praeparandae ut possint apponi et adsumi. Si autem ad ista vacare seruos dei certis interuallis temporum

ipsius infirmitatis necessitas cogit, cur non et apostolicis
praeceptis obseruandis aliquas partes temporum deputamus?

BIBLIOGRAPHY

THE LITERATURE OF THE 'DE CIVITATE DEI'

BERNHARD DOMBART has an interesting posthumous paper on the text. It is printed in Harnack & Gebhardt's 'Texte und Untersuchungen,' 1908, with the title: 'Zur Textgeschichte der Civitas Dei.' (Dombart having died before the publication, it was produced by Otto Stählin.)

The first printed edition appeared at Subiaco in 1467. Mentelin produced an important edition at Strasburg about the year following, which included the earliest commentary—that of Thomas Valois and Nicholas Triveth. This commentary is full in the earlier parts but meagre later. In 1522 J. L. Vives published the first edition which was made from a collation of the MSS., with a commentary of his own in which he attacked violently all the scholastic commentators. He makes many annotations. Some of them are amusing. We have interesting portraits of scholars like Sir Thomas More and Budé (Budæus), shrewd gibes that relieve a mass of detail, quips at scholastics, along with a defence of traditional religion against the unquiet spirit of Luther. With the comments of Vives are sometimes printed those of Leonard Coquæus (1661).

Of modern editions of the 'De Civitate Dei,' the best is that in the Vienna ' Corpus Scriptorum by E. Hoffmann. A smaller and later one, also in two volumes, by Dombart is useful. It lacks that elaborate table of contents which closes certain less important editions.

This table is not authoritative, but it is useful. Scholz gives an account of its origin.

118

In the late sixteenth century J. Healey made a fine translation. The folio edition of it issued in 1610 and 1620 gives also Vives' commentary. This translation (less the commentary) was recently reprinted in the 'Ancient and Modern Theological Library.' What purports to be the same appeared subsequently in three volumes in the Temple Classics. At the end of Vol. III we are told that Dr. Bussell, its editor, has rearranged and abridged it. He has done this without telling the reader where the cuts are made. Consequently all the references are useless except at the beginning, *e.g.* it has been compressed into eighteen books instead of twenty-two. It is difficult to know where we are, although the wording of the translation has not been changed. Another modern translation is that by Dr. Marcus Dods in the ' Library of the Fathers'—also there is one by Dr. Gee (London, 1894).

Literature on the 'De Civitate Dei' is large. Heinrich Scholz's 'Glaube und Unglaube in der Welt-geschichte' (Leipzig, 1911) is indispensable and everywhere interesting. It takes account of Reuter's view, but is independent. Bruno Seidel's thesis, ' Die Lehre des heiligen Augustinus vom Staate' is the most helpful single book. It is printed in Sdralek's 'Kirchen-geschichtliche Abhandlungen,' ix. 1 (1909). Hermann Reuter's 'Augustinische Studien' (Gotha, 1887) is illuminating; but his anti-hierarchical bias must be borne in mind. The third essay, that on the Church as the Kingdom of God, is the most important for the understanding of the ' De Civitate Dei.' But no part of it can be ignored.

Dorner's large book on Augustine ('Augustinus,' Berlin, 1873) has about one hundred pages bearing on the topics discussed here. It is important as it takes the view, followed by Ritschl and others, which makes Augustine the father of the Papacy.

Ritschl's Essay, 'Ueber die Methode der älteren Dogmengeschichte,' which appeared in the *Jahrbücher für Deutsche Theologie,* Bd. XVI, 191-214 (Gotha, 1871), is reprinted in the first volume of his 'Gesammelte Aufsätze,' pp. 147-169. It contains certain important statements about Augustine, which I have discussed. So also does the great work of Otto Gierke,' Das deutsche Genossenschaftsrecht.' These

119

maximise the clericalist side (in order to condemn it). The same is true of H. von Eicken in his book, 'Geschichte und System der mittelalterlichen Weltanschauung' (Stuttgart, 1887). Hertling severely, but not unfairly, attacked this in his 'Beiträge zur Philosophic.' Important essays on the subjects here discussed are hidden away in journals, *e.g.* Reuter laments the common ignorance of H. Schmidt's essays. They are published in the *Jahrbücher für Deutsche Theologie.* Vol. vi. pp. 197-255 (1861) contains that on 'Des Augustinus Lehre von der Kirche,' vols. vii. 237-281 and viii. 261-325 that on Origen and Augustine as apologists. Those are important. Ferdinand Kattenbusch is said to be the first to call attention to Augustine's identification of the Church with the apocalyptic kingdom. His 'Kritische Studien zur Symbolik' (the second essay) will be found in ' Theologische Studien und Kritiken' (Gotha, 1878). Feuerlein, who takes Augustine as a typical mediæval, wrote his essay, 'Ueber die Stellung Augustins in der Kirchen- und Culturgeschichte,' in Sybel's ' Historische Zeitschrift,' 1869, vol. xxii. 270. It is not otherwise valuable.

Edmond Boissier's 'Fin du Paganisme' has a good many pages bearing on this topic. So also an interesting thesis from Columbia University by E. Humphreys, 'Politics and Religion in the Days of Augustine.' On the philosophy of history there is Reinkens' rectorial address at Breslau (1865), to which I alluded in my second lecture. He was afterwards an Old Catholic bishop. This essay has been over-praised. Others are those of G. S. Seyrich, 'Die Geschichtsphilosophie Augustins nach seiner Schrift de Civitate Dei' (1891), and A. Niemann, 'Augustins Geschichtsphilosophie' (1895).

Two books that are indispensable are Joseph Mausbach's 'Die Ethik des heiligen Augustinus,' two volumes (Freiburg, 1909), and Ernest Troeltsch, ' Augustin, die christliche Antike und die Mittelalter' (1915). The latter is written in strong reaction against the view of Augustine as essentially mediæval. Mausbach writes an apologetic of S. Augustine against all who, like Ritschl, make him hostile to the State and to culture.

An American, Dr. Anson, wrote on the sources of the first ten books, and Dr. Frick has discussed those of the eighteenth.

A good account will be found in Dr. Cunningham's Hulsean Lectures (1885), 'S. Austin and his Place in the History of Christian Thought.' Dr. Carlyle in his 'History of Political Theories in the West' says surprisingly little. Professor Dunning says even less in his 'History of Political Thought.' There is an unsympathetic dissertation from Geneva by F. Thomas, 'S. Augustin, La Cité de Dieu' (1886). Harnack in the 'History of Dogma ' says some important things on the same lines as Ritschl and Gierke. Beard has some pages in his book on the Reformation. The former German Chancellor, Count Georg von Hertling, has a book on Augustine ('Der Untergang der antiken Kultur, Augustin,' 1902) in the series 'Weltgeschichte in Karakterbilden'; the pp. 98 and *sqq.* treat of the 'De Civitate Dei.' He declares this to be the most potent in influence of all S. Augustine's works. Hertling takes the view which I have taken in Lectures III and IV, and refuses to identify the two cities *sans phrase* with Church and State. Roundly he declares that of any hostility to the State on the part of the Church, Augustine knew nothing. A large book on Augustine ('Augustinus,' Paderborn, 1898) by Cardinal Rauscher, and published after his death, may be mentioned. Theo Sommerlad's two works, 'Das Wirtschaftsprogramm der Kirche des Mittelalters' (Leipzig, 1903) and 'Die wirtschaftliche Thätigkeit der Kirche in Deutschland' (Leipzig, 1910), carry to the farthest point the notion of Augustine as the author of a system of gigantic social reform. Robert-son's 'Regnum Dei' may also be consulted. Much use therein is made of Reuter.

APPENDIX

THE following passages from Vives may interest the reader: (II, 7.) 'Thus farre Lucian. We have rehearsed it in the words of Thomas Moore, whom to praise negligently, or as if one were otherwise imployed, were grossnes. His due commendations are sufficient to exceed great volumes. For what is he that can worthily lim forth his sharpness of wit, his depth of judgement, his excellence and variety of learning, his eloquence of phrase, his plausibility and integrity of manners, his judicious foresight, his exact execution, his gentle modesty and uprightness and his unmoved loyalty? Unlesse in one word he will say that they are all perfect, intirely absolute, and exact in all their full proportions? Unlesse he will call them (as they are indeed) the patterns and lusters, each of his kind? I speake much, and many that have not known Moore will wonder at me, but such as have, will know I speake but truth: so will such as shall either reade his workes or but heare or looke upon his actions: but another time shall be more fit to spred our sailes in this man's praises as in a spacious ocean, wherein we will take this full and prosperous wind and write both much in substance and much in value of his worthy honours, and that unto favourable readers.'

(VIII, 4.) ' It is a great question in our schooles whether Logic be speculative or practike. A fond question truly I thinke, and fellow with most of our philosophicall theames of these times, where the dreams of practice and speculation do nought but dull young apprehensions. . . . But these Schoolemen neyther know how to speculate in nature nor action, nor how the life's actions are to be ordered.'

(XI, 10.) ' Words, I thinke, adde little to religion, yet must we

122

have a care to keep the old path and received doctrine of the Church; for, divinity being so farre above our reach, how can wee give it the proper explanation?

All words are man's inventions for humane uses, and no man may refuse the old approved words to bring in new of his own invention; for whenas proprieties are not to bee found out by man's wit, those are the fittest to declare things by, that ancient use hath left us, and they that have recorded most part of our religion. This I say for that a sort of smattering rash fellowes impiously presume to cast the old formes of speech at their heeles, and to set up their owne masterships, being grossly ignorant both in the matters, and their bare formes, and will have it lawful for them at their fond likings to frame or fashion the phrases of the Fathers in matter of religion into what forme they list, like a nose of waxe.'

(XVIII, 18.) 'To create is to make something of nothing ; this God onely can do; as all the Divines affirme: but then they dispute whether hee can communicate this power unto a creature. Saint Thomas hath much concerning this; and Scotus seekes to weaken his arguments to confirme his owne; and Occam is against both, and Petrus de Aliaco against him: thus each one screweth the celestiall power into what forme he please. How can manners be amended, how can truth be taught, how can contentions be appeased as long as there is this confused obstinate jangling, and this haling too and fro in matter of Divinity, according as each man stands affected.'

(XIX, 21.) '*For we may not imagine man's, unjust decrees to be lawes; all men defining law to arise out of the fountaine of justice.*' (Cicero, *De Leg.* 1.)

Vives: 'It was not the people's command (saith he) nor Prince's decrees nor Judge's sentences, but the very rule of nature that gave original unto law. And again . . . Thus Tully out of Plato, and thus the Stoikes held against Epicurus, who held that nature accounted nothing just, but feare did. Seneca, *Epist.* 16. This holy law that lyeth recorded in every man's conscience, the civilians call right and reason. . . . So that Ulpian defineth law to be *ars aequi el boni*; an art of right and reason, making him

123

only a lawyer that can skill of this right and reason: and such that, as Tully said of Sulpitius, referre all unto equity, and had rather end controversies than procure them, that peace might generally be kept amongst men, and each be at peace with himselfe, which is the chiefe joy of nature.'

9 798889 421917